THE LAW OF THE SPIRIT OF LIFE IN CHRIST JESUS

By

Dwayne Norman

Empyrion Publishing
Winter Garden FL
EmpyrionPublishing.com

The Law of the Spirit of Life in Christ Jesus

Copyright © 2018 by Dwayne Norman

ISBN: 978-1491027189

Empyrion Publishing
PO Box 784327
Winter Garden FL 34778

EmpyrionPublishing.com

Unless otherwise noted, all Scripture quotations are from the New King James Version of the Bible.

All rights reserved. No part of this book may be reproduced, stored in a retrieval system, or transmitted in any form or by any means – electronic, mechanical, photocopy, recording, or any other, without permission in writing from the author.

Printed in the United States of America

Contents

1. Your Position Can Change Your Condition — 5
2. Can a Christian Lose His Salvation? — 27
3. The Power of Your Divine Rights — 41
4. The Courts of Heaven — 61
5. The Power of Resurrection Life — 87
6. Dual Citizenship — 113
7. The Ancient of Days — 127

CHAPTER 1

YOUR POSITION CAN CHANGE YOUR CONDITION

I want to share with you one of the greatest revelations that I've ever received from the Lord. It's found in Romans 8:2. God said, **"The law of the Spirit of life in Christ Jesus has made me free from the law of sin and death."** Now when it comes to receiving a revelation from the Lord, it is always progressive. He will speak a word into your spirit that will seem so real to you, like a light being turned on inside. You may have read the verse 100 times but it never came *alive* until now. That is called a rhema word or revelation (something revealed).

Just because the "spiritual" light is turned on in

your heart, doesn't mean you have all the light (understanding) on that revelation. It simply means, it is now real to you. It is not just head knowledge anymore. When it becomes real to you, in your heart, is when your faith will start working. Faith is in the heart not the head. Believe in your heart what you say will come to pass, and it will (Mark 11:23)!

Back in 1977, I was reading a book by the late John G Lake, and I was greatly inspired by his faith in God. Since then, I have gone to the internet and pulled up his testimony of how the Lord protected him during a great plague. This was posted by Everest John Alexander on October 18, 2015. Many have called it the Bubonic plague, but one minister said that through his studies, it was probably referred to as the Black Death, or a very bad strain of Malaria. Either way, many people died from it, but not Mr. Lake. He was there helping to bury the dead, and never contracted the disease.

"Now watch the action of the law of life. Faith belongs to the law of life. Faith is the very opposite of fear. Faith has the opposite effect in spirit, and soul, and body. Faith causes the spirit of man to become confident. It causes the mind of man to become restful, and positive. A positive mind repels disease. Consequently, the emanation of the Spirit destroys disease germs.

And because we were in contact with the Spirit of life, I and a little Dutch fellow with me went out and buried many of the people who had died from

emanation - an abstract but perceptible thing that issues or originates from a source.

the bubonic plague. We went into the homes and carried them out, dug the graves and put them in. Sometimes we would put three or four in one grave.

We never took the disease. Why? Because of the knowledge that the law of life in Christ Jesus protects us. That law was working. Because of the fact that a man by that action of his will, puts himself purposely in contact with God, faith takes possession of his heart, and the condition of his nature is changed. Instead of being fearful, he is full of faith. Instead of being absorbent and drawing everything to himself, his spirit repels sickness and disease. The Spirit of Christ Jesus flows through the whole being, and emanates through the hands, the heart, and from every pore of the body.

During that great plague that I mentioned, they sent a government ship with supplies and corps of doctors. One of the doctors sent for me, and said, "What have you been using to protect yourself? Our corps has this preventative and that, which we use as protection, but we concluded that if a man could stay on the ground as you have and keep ministering to the sick and burying the dead, you must have a secret. What is it?"

I answered, "Brother that is the 'law of the spirit of life in Christ Jesus.' I believe that just as long as I keep my soul in contact with the living God so that His Spirit is flowing into my soul and body, that no germ will ever attach itself to me, for the Spirit of God will kill it." He asked, "Don't you think that you had better use our preventatives?" I replied, "No, but doctor I think that you would like to experiment with me. If you will go over to one of these dead people and take the foam that comes out of their lungs after death, then put it under the microscope you will see masses of living germs.

You will find they are alive until a reasonable time after a man is dead. You can fill my hand with them and I will keep it under the microscope, and instead of these germs remaining alive, they will die instantly." They tried it and found it was true. They questioned, "What is that?" I replied, "That is 'the law of the Spirit of life in Christ Jesus.' When a man's spirit and a man's body are filled with the blessed presence of God, it oozes out of the pores of your flesh and kills the germs."

Suppose on the other hand, my soul had been under the law of death, and I were in fear and darkness? The very opposite would have been the result. The result would have been that my body would have absorbed the germs, these would have generated disease and I would have died.

You who are sick, put yourself in contact with God's law of life. Read His Word with the view of enlightening your heart so that you will be able to look up with more confidence and believe Him. Pray that the Spirit of God will come into your

soul, take possession of your body, and its power will make you well. That is the exercise of the law of the Spirit of life in Christ Jesus.'"

In case you have never heard about this awesome miracle, I wanted to share it with you at the beginning of this book. I want you to understand the reality of the law of the Spirit of life in Christ. Even though this phrase is a theological term in the book of Romans, I want you to see how practical it is. Learning what this phrase means is not just for more Biblical head knowledge. When we put it into practice, God's Spirit and power can be released to affect not only our bodies, but every area of our lives! The Lord does not want this to be only a theological study, but a reality in all that we do. My prayer is that this eternal Truth of Romans 8:2 will hit your spirit so forcefully and will penetrate so deeply into your heart that you will never be the same again! Instead of just looking at verse 2 of Romans 8, I want to look at several other verses as well.

Romans 8:1-4 says:
    1. "There is therefore now no condemnation to those who are in Christ Jesus, who do not walk according to the flesh, but according to the Spirit.
    2. For the law of the Spirit of life in Christ Jesus has made me free from the law of sin and death.
    3. For what the law could not do in that it was weak through the flesh, God did by sending His own Son in the likeness of sinful flesh, on account of sin: He condemned sin in the flesh,

The Law of the Spirit of Life in Christ Jesus

4. that the righteous requirement of the law might be fulfilled in us who do not walk according to the flesh but according to the Spirit."

The Bible says we do not have any condemnation because we are in Christ. II Corinthians 5:21 says we have been made God's righteousness in Christ. I know it may be hard to grasp, if you have not spent much time learning who Jesus is in you and who you are in Him, but God has made you as righteous as He is! That does not mean you cannot sin. Adam had no sin in him when he was created, but we found out he could still sin if he chose to. Every Christian needs to wake up to the fact that they are the righteousness of God in Christ; not because of their good deeds, but because of their <u>place in Him</u> (I Corinthians 1:30; 15:34). Good deeds are very important. They should be the outward results of our inward transformation. Let me say it again. Good deeds are very important!

We <u>must</u> obey the commandments of the Lord. But many have their understanding reversed. They think living a holy and clean life will make them a brand-new person inside, but it is just the opposite. Allowing the new creation you have been made in your spirit to come forth in your outer life, is a demonstration of holiness. As Christians, we are supposed to live from the inside out. The world (non-Christians) lives from the outside in. Whatever is on the news and going on around them will determine how they are on the inside. Their joy and peace is based on what is happening around them, but with us, it is based on who we are in Christ.

Look with me again at Romans 8:1. According to Wuest's Word Studies from the Greek New Testament, copyright by Wm. B. Eerdmans Publishing Company, he said, **"The words, "Who walk not after the flesh, but after the Spirit," are rejected by both Nestle and Westcott and Hort. Paul does not base his assertion of no condemnation to the saint upon the saint's conduct, but upon his <u>position in Christ</u>. His position in Christ has liberated him from the compelling power of the evil nature and made him a partaker of the divine nature, a new inner condition which produces in every saint a life which has for its motive, obedience to His commandments."**

It is very possible that in the original Greek in which Romans was penned, the phrase "Who do not walk according to the flesh, but according to the Spirit" was not in verse 1. Now don't get upset, it is still there, in verse 4. Think about this with me. When a lost person gets saved (accepts Jesus as his personal Lord and Savior), he or she becomes a brand new creation (person).

II Corinthians 5:17, 18 say:
    17. "Therefore, if anyone is in Christ, he is a new creation: old things have passed away; behold, all things have become new.
    18. Now all things are of God..."

The Bible teaches that man is spirit, soul and body (I Thessalonians 5:23). When I was born again, my body did not change (it was not made new) and my soul (mind, will, emotions) did not change (it was not made new). What became new was the real "Me", my spirit man. When I talk about our spirit man, I am using the word "Man" to refer to male and female persons who have been born again. According to verses 17 & 18, <u>all</u> things (in my spirit) have become new; therefore, <u>all</u> the old things are gone out of my spirit; and now, <u>all</u> the things in my spirit are of God. They are brand new! There is nothing inside me that the devil can condemn me for, since I am in Christ! I have a new nature in me (the life of God or the law of the Spirit of life in Christ)! The old nature (the Apostle Paul called him the old man-Romans 6:6) is dead and removed out of my spirit!

Even though I am a new man with a new nature (II Peter 1:4) I can still act like the old man if I choose to. I can still live and talk as if I had never been saved. That is why the Bible says to put on the new man. The Christian life is learning how to live from the <u>inside out</u>. We need to learn how to live out of all that God has put in our reborn spirits in Christ Jesus! When I got washed white as snow in Jesus' precious Blood, I was instantly made the righteousness of God. If the devil whispered in my ear and told me what an ungodly and sinful person I was, he would be lying. He would know, just like I should know that I do not have any condemnation in Christ, not because of me or my good works, but because of Jesus' death and resurrection; which incorporates all that God finished for me by His grace through the substitutionary sacrifice of Jesus. So, the foundation for having no condemnation is <u>my spiritual position or place in</u>

Him.

Of course, if I commit a sin, the devil will try to condemn me for it, but because of who I am in Christ, I have a right to call on Jesus as my advocate, repent to the Father, receive forgiveness and continue living a righteous life on this earth. Please always remember that the Holy Spirit does not condemn Christians if they sin. So quit saying that the Holy Spirit condemned me for this sin or for that sin! It is our heart that will condemn us if we sin. The Apostle John said:

19. "And by this we know that we are of the truth, and shall assure our hearts before Him.
20. For if our heart condemns us, God is greater than our heart, and knows all things.
21. Beloved, if our heart does not condemn us, we have confidence toward God." (I John 3:19-21)

The Holy Spirit does not condemn us for anything because Jesus bore all of our judgement at Calvary. Now, it is true, if you do not walk after the spirit but after the flesh, your heart will condemn you, but in your reborn spirit you are still God's righteousness in Christ. In John 16: 8, 9, the Lord Jesus said that the Holy Spirit will convict or convince the world (non-Christians) of sin (of the sin of rejecting Jesus as their savior). So, if you have messed up or missed it with the Lord, then your heart will condemn you, but that condemnation is the result of an unrenewed mind and a body that is yielding to sin. It is not because something has changed or gone wrong in your born again spirit. As I just said, if you and I do not walk after the spirit but after the flesh, our hearts will condemn us, but if the devil brings condemnation in the form of telling you that you are not really God's righteousness, then that's a lie; because <u>right now</u> you do not have any condemnation in your spirit man in Christ!

The reason the Holy Spirit can work through our spirits to renew our minds to God's Word and to train our bodies to walk in holiness is because all things have been made new in our spirits! You could say that we are under new management. Therefore, when you read Romans 8:1 out of the King James Bible and some other translations, please know and understand that at this very moment you do not have any condemnation in your spirit man because you are in Christ Jesus; not because you walk after the spirit and not after the flesh. How you walk and live in your outward life (through your mind and body) does not nullify or weaken your righteousness in Jesus.

Once again, if you use your mind and body to walk after the flesh, then your heart will condemn you; so just repent and receive forgiveness for that and keep putting on the new man every day. Yes, the Bible teaches us the importance of learning to walk after the spirit in Romans 8:4-5, 12-13; Galatians 5:16, 25, but as long as you are a Christian, your righteousness in your spirit will never ever change; so you will never have any condemnation in Christ! Any legitimate condemnation will not concern your reborn spirit, but it will be coming from your heart as it deals

Your Position Can Change Your Condition

with you concerning activities of your mind and body yielding to the flesh or to ungodly thoughts and actions. Let's look now at some other Scriptures that many Believers have been confused about.

6. "If we say that we have fellowship with Him, and walk in darkness, we lie and do not practice the truth.
7. But if we walk in the light as He is in the light, we have fellowship with one another, and the blood of Jesus Christ His Son cleanses us from all sin.
8. If we say that we have no sin, we deceive ourselves, and the truth is not in us.
9. If we confess our sins, He is faithful and just to forgive us our sins and to cleanse us from all unrighteousness.
10. If we say that we have not sinned, we make Him a liar, and His word is not in us.
1. My little children, these things I write to you, so that you may not sin. And if anyone sins, we have an Advocate with the Father, Jesus Christ the righteous.
2. And He Himself is the propitiation for our sins, and not for ours only but also for the whole world." (I John 1:6-10; 2:1-2)

I have a relationship and fellowship with God, like I do with my parents. If I disobey my parents, then my fellowship is severed. I'm walking in "Darkness" so to speak towards them, but my relationship is still intact. I am still their son, even though we may not be on good speaking terms. The

The Law of the Spirit of Life in Christ Jesus

same is true with our Heavenly Father. Sin can disrupt our fellowship with our Father, and if I have broken my fellowship and I say that I have not, then I would be lying. Wouldn't I? That is what verse 8 is saying. He said if you say you have no sin, you are deceiving yourself. It is just that simple. Do not say you have no sin in your life if you do.

I do not want to get you bogged down in the study of verbs and nouns, but there is something I want to share with you so that you will not receive an incorrect teaching. I would just ask that you judge for yourself based on the Word of God. Someone said the word "Sin" in I John 1:8 is a noun and not a verb, so it must be talking about having the sin nature that was in our spirits before we got saved. They assume because the word is not in a verb form, that it cannot be talking about sins you may be committing now. I heard a minister say that the word "Sin" in that verse can only be talking about the sin nature. Is that true? If it is then it has to agree with the rest of the Scriptures.

Think about this with me. If I robbed a bank yesterday, that would be the act of sinning (which would be a verb). If I did not repent, then today I would have sin (stealing, which would be the noun form) in my life. According to verse 8, if you then asked me if I had any sin (noun) in my life and I said no, that would be a lie. If I were to ask you if you have any sin in your life right now, I am not asking you if you have the sin nature we got from Adam; I am asking you if you have committed any sins in the past. So, I could ask, "Have you committed any sins (plural) in your life or do you have any sin (singular- the noun form) in your life."

If you have any un-confessed sin in your life, since you are not in the act of committing it anymore, that sin would be in the form of a noun. Therefore, verse 8 is not saying we still have the sin nature in our spirits. Just because it may be in the form of a noun does not mean that the only thing it could be is the old sin nature. If it was saying that, it would contradict other Scriptures. There are places in the Bible, such as Romans chapter six, where the word "Sin" is referring to the sin nature in the context of those Scriptures. Remember, the correct way to interpret the Bible is with the Bible, not with your experiences. Experiences are good as long as they line up with God's Word. The Word of God is final authority in our lives and always trumps experiences! If you are correctly explaining a verse from the Bible, it will always agree with all other Scriptures.

If the Apostle John meant in I John 1:8 that the word "Sin" is referring to the old nature of sin and death (the law of sin and death or the old man), the Holy Spirit through John would have contradicted His Word in the rest of this letter. He said in chapter 2, verses 6 & 9 that if we abide in Christ we won't sin. There is no way you are not going to sin if you still have the sin nature in your spirit. You cannot put off the old man if you are still the old man in your spirit. You must be a new man (all the old things have passed away) to put off the old man and to put on the new. The Apostle Paul said in Hebrews 9:14 that only the Blood of Jesus (through His death) could cleanse our conscience (which meant to give us a new nature).

The reason sinners sin, is because that is their nature. You are going to act according to your nature. Dogs bark because that is their nature. If you do not want them to bark then they must have a new nature. The sin nature is the nature of the devil we got through Adam. The only reason we can abide in Christ and He in us, is because we have His nature and the old one has been removed. Just because you have God's nature in you now, does not mean you will never sin again and it does not mean that you are incapable of sinning. He said in I John 2:1 that he wrote these things to us so that we <u>may not sin</u> (implying we do not have to), and if <u>we do sin</u> (implying you are still capable of sinning) we have an Advocate with the Father.

The Apostle Paul told us to awake to righteousness and sin not (I Corinthians 15:34). The Lord would not have commanded us not to sin unless we have a choice. Remember, our spirits were reborn, not our minds or bodies. If we do not keep our minds and bodies in line with God's Word, they will operate in the direction they were originally trained, through the old nature or old man that we once were.

I heard one minister say that I John chapter one was written to the lost and not to Christians. If you know anything about the New Testament, you know that the letter of I John is one of the epistles, and all of

Your Position Can Change Your Condition

the epistles are letters written only to the Church; only to Believers. God did not have John write one chapter to non-Believers and the rest to Believers! In I John 2:1, he addresses the recipients of this letter as "My little children", and in other places he reminds us that we are in Christ. Lost people are not in Christ; that is the wonderful privilege of being a Christian.

This particular minister quoted I John 1:9 and said that the Lord is talking about sinners confessing their sins and not Christians. Well first of all, a lost person would never ever remember all of the many sins he committed in his past so that he could confess them. The Bible says in Romans 10:9 that the only confessing a lost person needs to do is to confess Jesus as his Lord. In I John 1:8 he is saying that if you have sin in your life (which refers to sins you have committed in the past) and will not admit it, then you are lying; so from verse 8 he immediately go into verse 9 and tells you to confess those sins and receive your forgiveness. If verse 8 was referring to the nature of sin that was in your spirit before you got saved, you can't confess that to God and receive forgiveness for it.

In other words, the sin nature from Adam that came upon all of humanity (Romans 5:12) cannot be forgiven because it is not an act, it is heredity. Sins can be forgiven, but that sin nature was exterminated and destroyed out of your spirit through the death and resurrection of Jesus. When you confessed Jesus as your Lord, the Spirit of God immediately removed that sin nature out of your spirit and replaced it with

The Law of the Spirit of Life in Christ Jesus

God's Divine nature (eternal life and righteousness). Once again, the Bible does not tell lost people to ask God to forgive them for having the sin nature, it tells them to confess Jesus as their Lord; when they do, they receive a new nature (the law of the Spirit of life in Christ).

One more incorrect point this minister said was that Christians don't have to confess their sins because they have already been forgiven. I hope that you will get my book **"Grace, Faith and Rest"** for more teaching on understanding how grace and faith work together, resulting in supernatural rest.

It is very true that because of the grace of God bestowed upon us through the death and resurrection of Jesus: our sin nature has been destroyed, all of our sins past, present and future have been washed away by Jesus' Blood, our bodies have been completely healed by Jesus' 39 stripes and all financial lack and poverty have been removed out of our lives! We are totally free and redeemed! All these things have already been finished and done for us, but that does not mean you will automatically experience them done in your life right now. The Apostle Paul said in Romans 5:2 that we have to operate in faith to access God's grace so that we can experience and actually start enjoying all that Jesus finished for us at Calvary.

Yes, it is true that all of our sins have been washed away, but that does not mean that you never have to repent anymore and receive forgiveness. Just like healing has already been obtained for us, we still must release our faith to appropriate it or experience it in our bodies. You could say that forgiveness of sins is already in your spiritual bank account (grace account) but you still have to use your faith to make a withdrawal. The same is true for financial blessings, we have already been given Abraham's blessing and all spiritual blessings in Christ, but they will not automatically materialize without releasing or exercising our faith. You could say that our faith is our spiritual withdrawal slip.

So, back over in Romans chapter 8, Paul teaches us how to walk in the spirit by allowing the new man we are in Christ to rule and reign over our minds and bodies. He teaches us how to walk after the spirit and not after the flesh, but the reason we can do that is because of our <u>position in Christ</u>. Through our spiritual position, the Holy Spirit can change our outward condition. Therefore, if my fellowship is broken with the Lord, my relationship in Him is still good. I am still God's son. My position has not changed. In my spirit, I am still a new creation in Him. I just need to demonstrate that in my fellowship or behavior.

I want to make you aware of a heresy (false teaching) that is becoming more and more prevalent in churches today. It is not a new heresy. It is actually what the Apostle John was dealing with and having to correct by what he wrote in chapter 1, verse 6. He said, **"If we say that we have fellowship with Him, and walk in darkness, we lie and do not practice the truth."** Most Christians may not recognize the name of this false teaching, but it is called "Antinomianism". Please do not let the big word confuse you. It is the teaching that says a person may be living in sin and compromising with it, and at the same time have fellowship with God. This is a lie from hell. It's the devil's subtle way of corrupting the church.

<u>It's the doctrine of Balaam</u>. The Lord Jesus said to John, concerning the church in Pergamos, **"But I have a few things against you, because you have there those who hold the doctrine of Balaam, who taught Balak to put a stumbling block before the children of Israel, to eat things sacrificed to idols, and to commit sexual immorality."** (Revelation 2:14)

To summarize I John chapter 1, if you want to walk in fellowship with the God and experience the fullness of the blessing of the Gospel of the Lord Jesus Christ, then get the sin out of your life! He is not talking about the sin nature that was removed out of your inner man when you were born again, but all the other sins you thought you were getting away with. You may think you are doing ok because you are living in sin and nothing "bad" has happened to you yet. You are only deceiving yourself! God is not mocked! Whoever sows to the flesh will of the fresh reap corruption! God strongly told us in Deuteronomy 28:15, **"But it shall come to pass, if you <u>do not</u> obey the voice of the Lord your God, to observe carefully all His commandments and His statutes which I command you today, that <u>all these</u>**

curses will come upon you and overtake you." (Emphasis added throughout chapter)

Obviously, Balaam told the children of Israel that it was ok to disobey God's Word and live any way they wanted to live. He must have convinced them that they would be fine, and there would be no consequences (penalties) to their sin, but it resulted in their down fall. We need to learn a great lesson from them.

Again, I John 3:6, 9 say:
6. "Whoever abides in Him does not sin. Whoever sins has neither seen Him nor known Him.
9. Whoever has been born of God does not sin, for His seed remains in him; and he cannot sin, because he has been born of God."

According to Wuest Word Studies in the Greek New Testament, the phrase "Abides in Him" and "Does not sin" are referring to habitual actions. He said, **"Character is shown by one's habitual actions, not the extraordinary ones. The tense of the verbs is present, the kind of action, continuous, habitual. The unsaved person as a habit of life sins continually. The person who is abiding in Christ is not habitually sinning.**

Another scholar said that John did not teach that believers do not sin, but was speaking of a character, a habit. Wuest goes on to say, **"What John denies here is that a Christian sins habitually. He denies** that the life of a Christian is wholly turned towards sin as is that of the unsaved person. "His seed" refers to the principle of divine life in the believer. It is this principle of divine life that makes it impossible for a Christian to live habitually in sin, for the divine nature causes the child of God to hate sin and love righteousness, and gives him both the desire and the power to do God's will, as Paul said in Philippians 2:13, "for it is God who works in you both to will and to do for His good pleasure."

The Apostle was not teaching sinless perfection. He was not teaching that as soon as you get saved you will never sin again, and he was not teaching that you have to sin. He was teaching that if you abide (dwell continually) in Christ and yield to His nature within, you will not habitually sin. For you and I to sin, we have to yield to our fleshly (carnal) desires. We have to operate with selfish motives and attitudes. We have to temporarily stop walking in Christ and start walking according to the dictates of our flesh. Through God's Seed (Jesus) within our spirits we cannot sin as I John 3:9 says. In other words, you do not lie in Christ, you do not steal in Christ, and you do not commit adultery or murder in Christ. You have to yield to or walk in the flesh to do that. You have to listen to your flesh to sin. The Lord Jesus will not help you to sin. Now, I think that James 1:14, 15 will mean more to you.

14. "But each one is tempted when he is drawn away by his own desires and enticed.

15. Then, when desire has conceived, it gives birth to sin; and sin, when it is full-grown, brings forth death."

Notice He said we are tempted when <u>we</u> are drawn away by <u>our own desires</u>. Meaning, the devil can bring a temptation to us, but it will not succeed if we do not yield to fleshly desires. If we make up our minds that we are going to walk according to our position in Christ and not in the flesh, then the devil's temptations will always fail! That is what the Christian life is all about, learning to put on Christ, learning to put on the new man or living from the inside out! We should get better at it every day!

The Law of the Spirit of Life in Christ Jesus

CHAPTER 2

CAN A CHRISTIAN LOSE HIS SALVATION?

I want to bring something else to your attention. Some Christians believe that no matter how much they sin, it will never nullify or cancel out their salvation. They think, because of what a lot of preachers have told them, they have guaranteed passage to Heaven. They assume there is no sin they could commit that would jeopardize their relationship with the Father. They know that sin breaks their fellowship, but they think their relationship is unbreakable. Please don't be deceived! In the previous chapter I talked about how strong your relationship is in the Lord, and that if you sin, you break your fellowship with God. But, I was not teaching that it is impossible to break your relationship; it is just very, very difficult. What I am going to share with you in this chapter is a must for Christians to understand.

"Therefore, my beloved, as you have always obeyed, not as in my presence only, but now much more in my absence, work out your own salvation with <u>fear and trembling</u>." (Philippians 2:12)

What is all the fear and trembling about? As a Christian, if I believe I can live any way I want to and know I am still going to Heaven, then there is not a whole lot of fear and trembling to experience. Even if I know my sins have consequences, those consequences or penalties are still not as frightening as eternity in hell. But if it is possible for a child of God to lose his salvation, then that would definitely cause me to fear and tremble.

Romans 6:15 says, **"What then? Shall we sin because we are not under law but under grace? Certainly not!"** Just because I know my Father will forgive me if I mess up, I am not going to play with sin! I am not trying to see what I can get away with! I want to please God every day. I want to walk in the same intimate fellowship and holiness with my Father that Jesus did! Don't you? John 10:28 says:

"And I give them eternal life, and they shall never perish; neither shall anyone snatch them out of My hand."

Can a Christian Lose His Salvation?

The Lord Jesus spoke these very words. He is the one who has given us eternal life. I heard a very well-known minister say it is impossible for a Christian to lose his salvation because the Lord said, "They will never perish". Let me ask you a question. Who did the Lord say would never perish? This is not a trick question. He said "They". Who is "They"? They are those whom He has given eternal life. Well what must you do to get eternal life? You must *believe* Jesus died for you, arose from the dead and confess Him as your Lord (Romans 10:9, 10).

Therefore, those who believe, are the ones who will never perish. I am sure you would agree with that. Jesus cannot lie and God's Word is true, but what if you stop believing? You may be thinking right now, "Can you do that?" Remember, believing is operating in faith and faith is a decision you make. We all have free wills, don't we? A lost person makes a decision to believe on Jesus, when he does, he is born again. Yes, it is true, no other person or demon can take me out of God's hand, but I can take myself out of God's hand, if I chose to leave.

Of course, I do not choose to leave, but I still have that right or choice. If I decided not to believe anymore, God's not going to make me believe. He is not going to say, "You're going to Heaven whether you believe in Me or not. I will not allow you to quit believing in Jesus as your Savior." He will not brake or override your free will. It was free before you got saved, and it is still free while you are saved. You came into the Kingdom by believing in your heart and confessing with your mouth, and you can go out the same way. It is still your choice, so do not mess it up!

The good news is that it is extremely difficult to lose your salvation. It is not something you can do quickly. God is so merciful and compassionate. Jesus' precious Blood is so powerful. God will forgive and cleanse us of any sin, except rejecting Jesus. If a lost person says he refuses to believe in Jesus and will not acknowledge Him as his Lord, then God will not forgive him. God will not say I am going to let you into Heaven even though you will not accept My Son. Because Jesus said, in John 14:6, He is the <u>only</u> way to the Father. There are no exceptions!

I John 5:16, 17 say:
16. "If anyone sees his brother sinning a sin which does not lead to death, he will ask, and He will give him life for those who commit sin not leading to death. There is sin leading to death. I do not say that he should pray about that.
17. All unrighteousness is sin, and there is sin not leading to death."

I began studying this more, after reading something from Kenneth Hagin Sr. He said the Lord Jesus told him, when He appeared to him in a vision that the sin unto death in this particular verse was unto spiritual death. Even brother Hagin taught us not to follow after people's experiences, unless they agree with the Word of God. As I have already said God's Word always trumps experience! So get out your Bible, look up all these verses and study them for yourself. I do not believe what any preacher says unless it lines up with the Scriptures. I believe what the Lord told brother Hagin lines up with the Word, but you need to be convinced by the Scriptures yourself.

The Lord said, in verse 16, we could pray for our <u>brother</u>. A lost man is not my brother, but a fellow Believer is. He said I could pray for my brother concerning any sin he may commit and God will give him life, but He also said there is a sin my <u>brother</u> could commit (notice that he did not say that it was impossible to commit this sin) that I am not to pray for him about. And that sin would be, completely turning against Jesus and refusing to serve Him anymore. If he came to that place in his life, through unrepentant sins and disobedience to God's Word, where he decided, from his heart, that Jesus was not his Lord anymore, God would not forgive him. For God to forgive him would be the same as saying that you are still my child whether you believe on Jesus or not.

God will not forgive a person for not believing on the Lord. There is nothing He can do to help him if he refuses to believe. Operating in faith and making Godly decisions was not just to get into the Kingdom, but it is how we live for the rest of our lives. Without faith it is impossible to believe God (Hebrews 11:6).

Now there are other sins that can lead to physical death. We can pray for people about those. Let me remind you of some examples from the ministry of Jesus. In Jerusalem there was a pool called Bethesda. Every so often an angel would come down and stir up the water. Whoever stepped in first would be healed.

John 5:5-9, 14 says:
5. "Now a certain man was there who had an infirmity thirty-eight years.
6. When Jesus saw him lying there, and knew that he already had been in that condition a long time, He said to him, "Do you want to be made well?"
7. The sick man answered Him, "Sir, I have no man to put me into the pool when the water is stirred up; but while I am coming, another steps down before me."
8. Jesus said to him, "Rise, take up your bed and walk."
9. And immediately the man was made well, took up his bed, and walked. And that day was the Sabbath.
14. Afterward Jesus found him in the temple, and said to him, "See, you have been made well. <u>Sin no more</u>, lest a worse thing come upon you."
(Emphasis added throughout chapter)

The Lord made very clear to this man that he had that disease for thirty-eight years because of sin in his life. Do not ever think that sin does not have natural consequences. Think about it. All because of a sin he committed and never repented of, he was bound with a disease for thirty-eight years. As we progress in this book we are going to talk more about the legalities of our redemption. How the throne room of God is like a court room, and how that everything is based on laws (not Jewish laws). If you break God's spiritual laws and refuse to operate in them, then you are giving the devil legal entrance into your life, and that is what this man did at the pool of Bethesda.

Most of the time, according to the record we have in the four Gospels, Jesus did not tell people their sickness was the direct result of a sin they committed, but He did in this case. I know all sickness and disease is the result of Adam's sin, but that was not the sin Jesus was referring to here. If this man had not been healed, sometime later he could have died from that disease. His sin would have led unto death, but not spiritual death. Jesus forgave him when He healed him. The reason He forgave him is because his sin was not unto spiritual death.

He also forgave the woman caught in adultery, in John 8, because her sin was not unto spiritual death. In Luke 5, He forgave the paralytic who was let down through the roof because his sin was not unto spiritual death, but his sin could have been unto physical death. Also, Hezekiah was sick because of sin in his life (II Chronicles 32:24-26). Isaiah prophesied to him that he would die (physically), but he repented to God and He gave him 15 more years. Think about the example of the man who was committing incest (fornication) with his father's wife. He was a believer, part of the church at Corinth. Paul told the church to deliver him over to Satan for the destruction of his flesh, so his <u>spirit</u> would be saved. (1 Corinthians 5:1-5)

He was not saying this man needed to become a Christian. He was already saved, but Paul wanted to make sure he stayed saved. Well why would he need to do that if it is impossible to lose your salvation? Paul knew better than that didn't he? He knew if the man would not repent, he could end up spiritually lost. Listen, he had already committed the sin of fornication, but he was still saved (that shows the power of the new birth). The Bible did not say he immediately lost his salvation when he sinned. Paul knew if he continued in the direction he was headed, it would lead unto spiritual death. If this were the only choice, God would rather the man's spirit be saved, and he make it to Heaven, than his flesh be saved and he ends up in hell.

Please do not let people's experiences and visions confuse you about why people are in hell. God will forgive people of any sin they commit, except rejecting Jesus. The reason Christians go to Heaven is not because they never sin or mess up, but because they believe on Jesus as their Savior. The reason non-Christians go to hell is not because of their many sins, but because they reject Jesus. Now listen. Habitually sinning and not ever repenting can lead a person down the road to where they could reject the Lord, but a person will not be condemned to hell only because he stole some money, told a lie or had an unclean thought. Now stealing the money could be one of the many sins that might eventually lead the person to reject Jesus. If Christians have gone to hell, then they did not go there as a Christian. They lost Jesus along the way. Jesus is not living in anyone in hell. If Jesus lives in your heart when you die, you will go to Heaven! To be absent from the body is to be present with the Lord (II Corinthians 5:8).

Hebrews 6:4-6 say:
4. "For it is impossible for those who were once enlightened, and have tasted the heavenly gift, and have become partakers of the Holy Spirit,
5. and have tasted the good word of God and the powers of the age to come,
6. if they fall away, to renew them again to repentance, since they crucify again for themselves the Son of God, and put Him to an open shame."

Brother Hagin also said that Jesus told him that He (Jesus) is the Heavenly gift, and that also agrees with Scripture doesn't it (John 3:16)? In II Corinthians 9:15, Paul was thrilled with the financial gift the church was giving, but he began to the think about God's gift to us, His Son. He referred to Jesus as God's indescribable Gift! Tasting the Heavenly gift is about being born again. In other words, these verses strongly suggest that a baby Christian cannot lose his salvation. It must be a Believer who is filled with the Spirit, has spent enough time in the Word to know what he is doing and has operated in the gifts of the

Spirit (experienced God's power). Verse 6 says, "If they fall away..." Why would God say "If they fall away..." if it is impossible, no matter how much a person sins and denies Jesus, to fall away?

Revelation 3:5; 22:19 say:
5. "He who overcomes shall be clothed in white garments, and I will not blot out his name from the Book of Life; but I will confess his name before My Father and before His angels.
22. And if anyone takes away from the words of the book of this prophecy, God shall take away his part from the Book of Life, from the holy city, and from the things which are written in this book."

Isn't great to know that your name is in the Book of Life? Revelation 20:15 says, **"And anyone not found written in the Book of Life was cast into the lake of fire."** This is definitely the Book you want your name in! But the Lord Jesus said it is possible to have your name blotted out. Since everyone who has confessed Jesus as his or her Lord is in the Book of Life, then how could it be impossible for a Christian to lose his salvation if his name can be blotted out of this Book? Let me show you what I Corinthians 6:9-11.

9. "Do you not know that the unrighteous will not inherit the kingdom of God? Do not be deceived, neither fornicators, nor idolaters, nor adulterers, nor homosexuals, nor sodomites,
10. nor thieves, nor covetous, nor drunkards,

nor revilers, nor extortioners will inherit the kingdom of God.

11. And such were some of you. But you were washed, but you were sanctified, but you were justified in the name of the Lord Jesus and by the Spirit of our God."

To understand this, you must remember that Paul is talking to the church at Corinth. He is talking to Christians. If you are a Christian, you have inherited God's Kingdom. It is already yours. You are not getting it one of these days in the sweet by and by. Colossians 1:13 says we have been (not going to be) translated out of the devil's kingdom into God's Kingdom. We are not part of this world anymore. We are living in the Kingdom every day. So, He is not telling people who are already in the Kingdom that they will not be able to get into the Kingdom. He is really talking about how to keep from being removed out of the Kingdom, or having your name blotted out of the book of life. Again, it is called working out your own salvation with fear and trembling.

In verse 9, he is identifying a type of people by the term "Unrighteous", more than a specific sin someone committed. The "Unrighteous" are the lost. The "Righteous or just" are Christians. When you say the just or righteous shall live by faith, you are saying the Christian shall live by faith. You are identifying a type or class of person. In verse 11, he confirms that by saying, and such were some of you, but now you are justified (the righteous) in Jesus' Name.

He is saying that you once committed these sins when you were part of the type called the "Unrighteous or lost", but you got saved and became the "Righteous"; so do not go back to your old life style. If you do go back and continue that way without repenting, it is possible, at some point in time; that the result could be spiritual death. I believe the Word teaches that losing your salvation is very difficult and not something that could happen overnight, but it is still possible. I say that because the new birth, the born again experience is so awesome and powerful!

All of hell could not stop the Father from raising Jesus from the dead! The devil and all his demons could not stop Jesus from passing from spiritual death unto spiritual life! He was made alive so we could be made alive together with Him. The entire kingdom of darkness could not stop us from being again once we made the decision to accept Jesus as our Lord! The devil could not override what the Holy Spirit did in our inner man. The law of the Spirit of life in Christ Jesus set us free from the law of sin and death!

The reality of the new birth was a great revelation to the Apostle Paul. In Acts 20:26, he said, **"Therefore I testify to you this day that I am innocent of the blood of all men."** Paul was almost like a hit man for the devil before he got saved. It was his goal in life to get rid of Christians and throw them in jail. But he understood what it meant to be in

Can a Christian Lose His Salvation?

Christ and to have <u>no</u> condemnation for sin. He knew his past was gone forever and he had a brand new life; a new nature, God's nature. The law of the Spirit of life in Christ Jesus has truly made us free from the law of sin and death! Let's stay free! Always believe God's Word and obey it! We need to seek the Lord continually for more direction from His Word to walk deeper and fuller in His eternal Truth every day. In my time of studying and meditating the Word, I am also examining myself in the light of the Scriptures to make sure what I believe always lines up with the Scriptures. We should never be afraid to receive correction from the Word. Man's opinions do not matter, but what God's holy Word says does matter! We need to fear God and tremble at His Word (Isaiah 66:2)!

The Law of the Spirit of Life in Christ Jesus

CHAPTER 3

THE POWER OF YOUR DIVINE RIGHTS

I want us to go back to Romans 8:1-2 and look at it in the Amplified Bible for a minute.

"Therefore there is now no condemnation [no guilty verdict, no punishment] for those who are in Christ Jesus [who believe in Him as personal Lord and Savior].

For the law of the Spirit of life [which is] in Christ Jesus [the law of my new being] has set you free from the law of sin and death."

One day when I was meditating on these verses I got to thinking about the word "Law" in verse two. Why did the Holy Spirit have Paul call the Spirit of

The Law of the Spirit of Life in Christ Jesus

Life in Christ Jesus a law? If you read that verse without the word "Law" then it would say that the Spirit of Life in Christ Jesus has set me free from sin and death, and you know what? That would be 100% true; but he did not say it that way. Every Word of God in the Bible is relevant and necessary. So, He must have had a reason for calling the Spirit of Life in Christ a law.

I think that some Christians believe that the "Law" He is referring to is some kind of Jewish law, but it has absolutely nothing to do with the Jewish laws. I could see how someone might make that mistake if they think that the only laws which exist are Jewish laws. If you can't see past the Jewish laws then you will never understand the law of the Spirit of Life in Christ. Whenever the Bible uses the word "Law" it does not always refer to the Jewish laws.

I can give you at least six different laws we need to know about. First, there are the Jewish laws which the children of Israel lived under in the Old Covenant, but through Jesus' sacrifice, He fulfilled those laws for us, and as Christians we are not living under them now. We are under grace and are living in God's new and eternal Blood Covenant. There are civic laws, laws that tell us it is illegal to break the speed limit, to run a red light or to rob a bank; including many other laws beside those. There are natural laws, and some of them are the law of gravity, the laws of physics and the laws of aerodynamics.

There are also spiritual laws and forces. The devil's kingdom of darkness operates by spiritual laws and forces, the law of sin and death being the chief law; included in that would be fear, doubt, lust, strife, unforgiveness, envy and all that makes the kingdom of darkness function. God's Kingdom of Light operates by spiritual laws and forces, the law of the Spirit of Life being the chief law; within that you have faith, joy, love, forgiveness, sowing and reaping and other great laws and forces.

One more very important law that we need to remember, is what we live and govern our lives by, and that is the Word of God. We are going to find out that a law is something that always works; therefore God's Holy Word is spiritual law to every Believer. It always works! Since our God is a God of integrity and it is impossible for Him to lie, then His Word is unbreakable spiritual law to us! Here is a dictionary definition of the word "Law".

"A formulation describing a relationship that is presumed to hold between or among phenomena for all cases in which the specified conditions are met."

To give you a more concise definition of a law, as I have already mentioned, would be to say that a law always works. According to the dictionary, a law describes a relationship between phenomena that hold for all cases, but notice, that it is for all cases where the specified conditions are met. In other words, a law always works and will never fail unless another condition or law is introduced which can override and supersede the original law. Let me give you an example. The law of gravity is a law because it always works. Someone tested it enough and came to the conclusion that whatever goes up on this earth will always come down; that is why it is called a law.

The interesting thing about the law of gravity is that other laws can override it, making it appear that the law of gravity is not working; but we know it is. If you introduce the laws of aerodynamics, the law of lift and the law of thrust into the situation, you can supersede the law of gravity and lift off the ground in a plane and fly. While you are flying in the plane, you may think that the law of gravity is not working, but it is. You are simply overriding it with other laws you have set in motion. If you turn off the plane's engine, you will quickly realize that the law of gravity is still in operation.

The laws of the natural realm can be superseded by other natural laws, and the spiritual laws in the devil's kingdom can be superseded by God's spiritual laws, but the great news is, the spiritual laws of the Kingdom of God cannot be superseded by any other laws or forces. They are the highest of all laws and forces. So if you can learn how to put them to work in your life, the devil does not have anything he can use to override them, and to keep you from succeeding in life. The reason the law of the Spirit of Life in Christ always works is because every time a lost person believes that God raised Jesus from the dead and confesses Him as his Lord, he is automatically born again, and there is nothing the devil can do to stop it.

The devil cannot stop the Spirit of Life in Christ from coming into a person and giving him eternal life or setting him free from the nature or law of sin and death. After you received and confessed Jesus as your Lord, the devil could not come along and say, "I will not let you be saved". It was too late, the law of the Spirit of Life already superseded the law of sin and death and another person was born again. The law of sin and death can never override law of the Spirit of Life in Christ Jesus. Receiving the new birth is the greatest of all miracles, but it is not the only benefit for operating in this great spiritual law of God. Do you remember the story I shared about John G. Lake at the beginning of this book?

He was supernaturally protected from the Bubonic plague wasn't he? Obviously, the law of sin and death contains more than just spiritual death. All the curse of the law, all sin and death, all sickness, disease, poverty, lack and fear came into this earth through Adam when he sinned and allowed the law of sin and death to come into his spirit. He then passed it on to all of those he represented which was the entire human race. When you really believe and operate in the law of the Spirit of the Life in Christ then nothing in the law of sin and death has a <u>legal right</u> to manifest itself in your life. It would have to override the law of the Spirit of Life to do that. I hope that you are getting excited about this! I am talking about the power of our Divine rights or you could say the legalities of our redemption in Christ. If you can get good, so to speak, at releasing your faith, like Mr. Lake was, in activating God's spiritual laws then you will always experience victory in every area of your life!

If you never give place to the devil through ungodly actions, behaviors, attitudes and especially through speaking words contrary to God's Word (which is spiritual law), then you will never give him a legal entrance into your life. If you never give him a legal entrance into your life then he does not have any authority or power to enforce his will on you! And let me say this also. It does not matter what your ungodly relatives did in your past bloodline! You could say that our worst past relative was Adam, who hurt humanity the most, but since we are free from his sin and the consequences of it by the Blood of Jesus, then we are definitely free from all the sins and their penalties (what some call generational curses) which were manifested in the lives of any of our past relatives after Adam. Because of what Jesus (by His grace) finished for us at Calvary, we do not have to repent for Adam's sin, much less the sins of any of our past relatives!

As a Christian who is walking and living in Christ, the devil does not have any authority or power to put on you the sickness, disease, poverty and fear that he may have put on your tenth grandfather back.

The Power of Your Divine Rights

I am just picking out that number for an example here. It could refer to any of your past grandfathers. If your tenth grandfather back opened up a legal door to the devil in his life, that was his fault, not yours! Yes, I know that the devil may try to make you suffer the mess your tenth grandfather suffered and that was passed on to his children, but because you are a Christian and you know your legal rights in Christ, you can put a stop to that! You should know that as a Believer, who is not giving Satan legal place in your life, that he cannot make you take or suffer anything that your past bloodline relatives allowed him to put on them!

The sins they committed back then gave Satan legal entrance into their lives, but if you are a Believer and have not committed those sins then he has no legal grounds to attack you. I did not say that he will not try to attack you illegally. He will attack you whether it is legal or illegal just to see if you will allow him access in your life, but I said that he does not have any <u>legal right</u> to attack you. Now, if you are not a Believer, it does not matter whether you committed those same sins or not because you are still living in the devil's kingdom and through the law of sin and death in your spirit, your whole life is wide open to him. If what I just said describes you, then you need to get saved immediately! According to Romans 10:9, right now ask and receive the Lord Jesus into your heart and life, believe in your heart that God raised Him from the dead and confess Him as your Lord! If you will do that and believe it with all your heart then you will be instantly born again and removed out of Satan's legal jurisdiction!

I pray that as you read the Word of God in this book, the Holy Spirit will give you a greater consciousness and reality of the spirit realm; that what takes place in the natural realm in your life, your spouse, your children, your relatives, your friends and our governmental leaders is the result of what is happening, whether good or bad, in the spirit realm. Also, I pray that the Lord will give you a deeper and clearer understanding of how spiritual laws and forces work, and the importance of becoming very developed in operating in God's Divine laws. Please keep this ever in the forefront of your mind that <u>everything in the spirit realm is legally based</u>. Once again, I am not talking about Jewish laws but spiritual laws.

I remember hearing a message from Kenneth Hagin Sr. about going to the City of Faith hospital in Tulsa, Oklahoma to pray for a 39 year old man who was in a coma and was dying. Brother Hagin said that he and the young man's pastor prayed together for about an hour in tongues for him, then the Lord spoke through Brother Hagin. The Lord said that spiritual laws had been set in motion and there was nothing that could be done for the young man. Of course, the Lord was talking about negative spiritual laws being set in motion in the man's life. He also said to release his spirit so that he could go on to Heaven. So, the man died, never making it to 40 years old. I praise

God that he went to Heaven, but he could have enjoyed a much longer life. Brother Hagin also said that he attended his funeral and got into a conversation with the young man's brother. His brother said that this young man, since they were kids, always confessed that he would never live to be 40 years old, and that is exactly what he got. He enforced those negative words long enough that he finally had what he said.

Wow, what a sad, yet sobering story! It really causes you to examine your life and to make sure that you have not been opening any doors of your life to the devil. Now, let me remind you of a couple of important Scriptures here.

"Death and life are in the power of the tongue, And those who love it will eat its fruit." (Proverbs 18:21)

"But I say to you that for every idle word men may speak, they will give account of it in the day of judgment.
For by your words you will be justified, and by your words you will be condemned." (Matthew 12:36-37)

If you never learned this then please learn it now. The words of your mouth are containers. They can contain faith or fear, love or hate; it is your decision. God set the example for us by speaking the worlds into existence. He did not think the worlds into existence; He spoke them into manifestation, didn't He? In Mark 11:23, the Lord Jesus told us that we can have what we say, not what we think, if we believe in our hearts that what we say will come to pass; and that is actually one of God's spiritual laws. If you are speaking words contrary to God's Word, like saying that you always have back pain, when God's Word (spiritual law) says that you have been healed by Jesus' stripes (I Peter 2:24), you will probably always have back pain. Even if you did not believe what you said when you first started speaking those negative words, by continuing to say them long enough, at some point they can sink down in your spirit (heart) and then you will start believing what you are saying, and it can come to pass.

When that happens, you have set spiritual laws into motion to work against you. You would be giving Satan a legal right to work in your life, and you would be allowing him to use your authority (that God gave you in Christ) to keep your back in pain all of the time. Think how powerful that verse is which says that life and death are in the power of the tongue. It is saying that you have a decision to make. You get to choose which one you want. Do you want death in your life or do you want life? If you do not want death in your life and family, if you do not want sickness and financial lack, and if you do not want strife and stress among your spouse and children, then quit speaking it!!

<u>You do not get what you want just because you</u>

<u>want it</u>! You get only what you say out of your mouth that you believe in your heart will come to pass! If what you are saying does not agree with what you want then you need to change what you are saying! Also, in Matthew 12:37, He said that by your words you will be justified or condemned. The words justified and condemned sound like legal words or words you would hear in a court room, don't they? I just want to touch on this briefly before we get to the next chapter on the Courts of Heaven. If you have not noticed before, the Bible paints a word picture of God's throne room as set up like a modern day court room. Now, understanding this is important to receiving a greater revelation that everything in the spirit realm is legally based. Just like in a courtroom you have the presiding judge. In God's courtroom He is the eternal presiding Judge. He is the judge over all creation and all beings, and as a true judge of integrity, He will not make any judgement that would break His spiritual law (the Word of God).

I said that to say this. <u>One of the major secrets to a successful Christian life is discovering your personal authority</u>! Your personal authority is totally connected to your understanding of the legalities of your redemption, or your understanding of the benefits and privileges that you have in Christ. If you would like more in-depth teaching about your identity in Christ, please get our book "IN CHRIST: True Purpose, True Peace and True Fulfillment" from our website: dwaynenormanministries.org. We also have 70 (13 minute) audio messages on youtube.com entitled "Your Identity in Christ" under the name Dwayne Norman, and we have 25 (13 minute) audio messages entitled "Have You Found Yourself". I hope that you will listen to all 95 of these messages.

Let me give you an example of understanding your personal authority through the knowledge of the workings of God's spiritual laws. Your personal authority (from God) is the right you have been given to execute God's spiritual laws. That is what Jesus did when He rebuked the storm and it stopped in Mark 4:35-41. The devil instigated the storm in hopes of killing the Lord and His disciples, but the only laws that he had authority to execute were those in his kingdom; such as the law of sin and death and the law of fear. The Lord had the right to operate in the Law of the Spirit of Life and the law of faith which always override the law of sin and death.

When you set God's spiritual laws into motion, you release His authority, power and dominion into the situation. The devil did not have a chance and Jesus knew that; that's why the Lord took a nap; there was nothing to worry about. Also, in that story, the devil was not only trying to kill all of them in the boat, but he was also working through the disciples to aid in his plan. The disciples did not realize the devil was using them against themselves and the Lord. The devil is influencing people today to say and do a lot of things that are contrary to God's Word, and they are not even aware of it.

The Power of Your Divine Rights

In Mark 4:38, Jesus' disciples said, "...Teacher, do You not care that we are perishing?" After Jesus got up and rebuked the storm, He then rebuked His disciples for operating in fear. You could also say that they were setting the law of fear into operation, siding with the devil to kill everyone in the boat. Despite all of the demonic laws and forces being released against Jesus, they still failed! Jesus had what He said, and they all came over safely to the other side! Here is the moral of the story. If the devil and every demon in hell are coming against you, they will always lose when you are operating in the law of the Spirit of Life in Christ Jesus!!

There is absolutely nothing Satan and his demons can do to stop the law of the Spirit of Life in Christ Jesus from working in your life and keeping you free from the law of sin and death; that's why the Bubonic plague instantly died when it touched Mr. Lake's hand! When the law of sin and death touched the law of the Spirit of Life in his skin, that deadly disease in the law of sin and death died immediately! Praise God forever!! I am so glad that the law of the Spirit of Life in Christ is the law of my new being!! As Christians, we do not have to subjugate ourselves to the law of sin and death! That law does not govern and control our lives anymore! That also means that fear, doubt, lust, sin, poverty, sickness and disease do not have a legal right to operate in our lives!

If you will go back to Deuteronomy 28 and read verses 15-68, you will get a good description of all that was included in the curse of the law that we are redeemed from. Everything in the curse of the law that we are free from came upon mankind as a result of Adam allowing the law of sin and death to enter this earth. So, to be free from the law of sin and death is to be free from the curse of the law and all curses; which would include any generational curses! When it comes to the Word of God and all of His spiritual laws, we should be like highly successful attorneys going into the court room to defend their clients, they go in knowing the legal system backwards and forwards. They are not ignorant of the laws of the land are they? They know what they want their clients to receive from the judge, and they know that the judge's verdict will be totally dependent upon how well they have prepared their legal defense.

Once again, in our daily Christian life, we should operate like very successful "Spiritual" attorneys in the court room of Heaven. We need to press into the realities of God's Kingdom and our citizenship in it, and continually seek to know God's Word (His spiritual law) backwards and forwards so to speak. When you have great confidence in what the Word says that Jesus has already done for you at Calvary, it will inspire great faith to step out and receive whatever you need from the Lord. You need to realize that the Word you are standing on is God's spiritual law and it cannot be broken, and there is nothing the devil can do to stop it from working for you! Just like a good attorney, you have to believe in the law; in your case, God's spiritual law and all the laws that govern His Kingdom. Let's become an expert in who we are in Christ and how to daily operate in the law of the Spirit of Life in Him!

When you think about the Word of God as spiritual law, I believe this will help you. II Corinthians 8:9 says that Jesus bore our poverty so that we might be made rich. That is a law! You cannot change that! Even if you are not experiencing financial prosperity, what God said in that verse is still true. Yet, Christians will doubt what that verse says, because they cannot pay their bills. When they do not believe and act on God's Word, they are refusing to operate in God's spiritual laws, and therefore defaulting into the devil's spiritual laws. They are giving the devil permission to steal their money. Think about this also. When it comes to our natural laws, people never doubt them. I never hear people say, "I doubt that the law of gravity will work today." Even if we do not understand everything about gravity, we still believe that it is a law and will always work.

Even if the money you need is not manifested yet, do not quit believing in God's laws of prosperity. I can do all things through Christ which strengthens me (Philippians 4:13) is a law; that means it always works, whether you are experiencing it or not. By Jesus' stripes we were healed (Isaiah 53:3-5; I Peter 2:24) is a law, even if you do not feel healed. My feelings will not change the law of gravity, and my feelings will not change the law of healing. Based on

The Law of the Spirit of Life in Christ Jesus

the Scriptures, healing is God's will for everyone; whether everyone will receive healing or not. As you know, God does not want anyone to parish (John 3:16; I Timothy 2:4; II Peter 3:9); that is a law, even though there are people who choose not receive God's free gift of salvation. **God's will is not determined by what people receive or do not receive, it is determined by what His Word says, and what His Word says is law.**

Remember, all of God's authority and power accompany His Word to bring it to pass. When you and I believe what God's Word says, and declare it true in our lives; our faith activates God's Word to work as spiritual law in our lives, and there is nothing the devil can do to override it. On the other hand, if you speak contrary to God's spiritual law then you are giving Satan a legal right to come in and mess your life up. God's Word will always work for you when you believe and obey it, and the devil (sickness, lack, fear, doubt, depression, anger, lust and evil) will never be able to get a foothold in your life! So, he is hoping that you will give him an opening.

I want us to look at a natural example now that will help to illustrate this spiritual Truth. I believe that understanding the origin of the authority and power our earthly rulers (police officers, etc…) operate in will give us a better understanding of the authority and power we orperate in as God's spiritual police officers. Romans 13:1-4 and I Peter 2:13-14 say:

1. "Let every soul be subject to the governing authorities. For there is no authority except from God, and the authorities that exist are appointed by God.
2. Therefore whoever resists the authority resists the ordinance of God, and those who resist will bring judgment on themselves.
3. For rulers are not a terror to good works, but to evil. Do you want to be unafraid of the authority? Do what is good, and you will have praise from the same.
4. For he is God's minister to you for good. But if you do evil, be afraid; for he does not bear the sword in vain; for he is God's minister, an avenger to execute wrath on him who practices evil.
13. "Therefore submit yourselves to every ordinance of man for the Lord's sake, whether to the king as supreme,
14. or to governors, as to those who are sent by him for the punishment of evildoers and for the praise of those who do good."

Many Christians believe that all the governmental leaders in our nations are appointed by God, but that is not what these verses say. It is true that all authority comes from the Lord because He is the source of all power and authority. It all originally came from him, but many including the devil have used authority to promote evil and wickedness; those who have done this were not appointed by God.

Romans 13:1 says that those authorities which exist were appointed by God, but then in verses 3 and 4 the Holy Spirit gives us a very good description of what those authorities should be doing if they are truly appointed by God. In verse 3, Paul tells us that these rulers (which are appointed by God) are not a terror to good works, but to evil; so my conclusion is that any rulers who are promoting evil and not good are not appointed by God.

Even in verse 4 he said that these rulers (which are appointed by God) are avengers to execute wrath on him who practices evil. It sounds to me, based on what the Bible says that ungodly, evil dictators are not appointed by God because the rulers which God appoints will promote righteousness and godliness. Also, in Romans 13:4 it says, **"...But if you do evil, be afraid; for he does not bear the sword in vain..."**. I want you to notice the word "Sword" in that verse. I know that our police men and women do not use swords, but they use guns; either way the sword represents their authority and power to enforce the laws of the land. Therefore, in the natural realm, without a legal right, our rulers do not have authority to enforce anything against us. In the spirit realm it works the same way. When it comes to the devil, without a legal right, he does not have authority or power to enforce anything against us. As Christians, the devil will still attack us illegally, but if we are not giving him any legal place in our lives then he will always lose, and we will always quench every dart with our shield of faith (Ephesians 6:16).

CHAPTER 4

THE COURTS OF HEAVEN

I have heard a lot of teaching lately on the courts of Heaven. In my opinion (because we all are constantly learning and growing), much of the teaching is very good and Scriptural, and has been a great blessing to me; but there are a couple of things that I wanted to address from the Word of God in this chapter. Before I touch on those things, let's see what the Bible has to say about the courts of Heaven. Also, what I have shared with you in the first three chapters of this book is of vital importance in correctly understanding how the courts of Heaven function; so if you skipped to this chapter, please go back and read the first three. I want to give you a few Scriptures that talk about the courts of Heaven, and then we are going to hear what

The Law of the Spirit of Life in Christ Jesus

the prophet Daniel had to say.

"Blessed is the man You choose, and cause to approach You, that he may dwell in Your <u>courts</u>. We shall be satisfied with the goodness of Your house, of Your holy temple." (Psalm 65:4)

"For a day in Your <u>courts</u> is better than a thousand. I would rather be a doorkeeper in the house of my God than dwell in the tents of wickedness." (Psalm 84:10)

"Those who are planted in the house of the Lord shall flourish in the <u>courts</u> of our God." (Psalm 92:13)

"Give to the Lord the glory due His name; bring an offering, and come into His <u>courts</u>." (Psalm 96:8)

"Enter into His gates with thanksgiving, and into His <u>courts</u> with praise…" (Psalm 100:4)

If we start by looking in the book of Daniel, I believe that we can lay a foundation for observing God's throne room as a courtroom. This is a vision which the Lord gave to Daniel about some future events that would come to pass. I want us to look at some things in this particular chapter that describes God's throne as a courtroom. I am not looking at these Scriptures to teach on the book of revelation or end time events, because I am still talking about the power of our Divine rights which I discussed in the previous chapter. By understanding how God's spiritual courtroom functions, we will receive a deeper consciousness and a greater reality in our lives that everything in the spirit realm is legally based.

9. "I watched till thrones were put in place, and the <u>Ancient of Days</u> was seated; His garment was white as snow, and the hair of His head was like pure wool. His throne was a fiery flame, its wheels a burning fire:
10. A fiery stream issued and came forth from before Him. A thousand thousands ministered to Him; ten thousand times ten thousand stood before Him. <u>The</u> <u>court</u> was seated, and the <u>books were opened</u>.
13. I was watching in the night visions, and behold, <u>One like the Son of Man, coming with the clouds of heaven! He came to the Ancient of Days, and they</u> <u>brought Him near before Him</u>.
14. Then to Him was given dominion and glory and a kingdom, that all peoples, nations, and languages should serve Him. His dominion is an everlasting dominion, which shall not pass away, and His kingdom the one which shall not be destroyed.
21. I was watching; and the same horn was making war against the saints, and prevailing against them,
22. <u>Until the Ancient of Days came, and a judgment was made in favor of the saints of the Most High, and the time came for the saints to</u>

possess the kingdom.
26. But the court shall be seated, and they shall take away his dominion, to consume and destroy it forever. (Daniel 7:9-10, 13-14, 21-22, 26 emphases added throughout chapter)

Up until now we have been talking about the legalities of our redemption; how the devil legally usurped man of his authority and how the Lord Jesus legally got it back for us. One proof of that is in what the Lord said to the Church after he arose from the dead.

"And Jesus came and spoke to them, saying, "All authority has been given to Me in heaven and on earth,
Go therefore and make disciples of all the nations, baptizing them in the name of the Father and of the Son and of the Holy Spirit,
Teaching them to observe all things that I have commanded you; and lo, I am with you always, even to the end of the age." Amen (Matthew 28:18-20)

The Lord got back the authority that the devil got from Adam, but He did it legally didn't He? As Believers, we now have all authority in Heaven, on earth and under the earth or in Hell! Now that we are in Christ, we have all authority and power over Satan and his entire kingdom! In the spirit realm the Lord did all this legally for us, and the way we operate in all this authority and power is through putting God's spiritual laws to work in our lives. Now, getting back to Daniel's vision; at least twice in that seventh chapter we read, it uses the word "Court". In the King James Bible it uses the word "Judgment" in the place of the word "Court". The word "Judgment" is a legal term and would also refer to the seat of judgment in a courtroom; so the word "Judgment and court" would be very synonymous.

What I like about the teaching I have heard on the courts of Heaven, is it helps you to become more cognizant and aware that important things are always taking place in the spirit realm, and that you and I have a very important part in that. Whether you realize it or not, ministers have been teaching for years about what is happening in the spirit realm through our prayers and operating in God's spiritual laws without using the phrase "Courts of Heaven". This teaching really is not new, we are just looking at it through different words and phrases, but that is good because it helps to give more light and understanding to us about our rights in Christ.

So, when God opened up Daniel's spiritual eyes to see His throne room, he described it as a courtroom; with the Ancient of Days (almighty God) being the judge. I John 2:1 says that we have an advocate (attorney) with the Father, Jesus Christ the righteous. Our Savior is also our spiritual attorney. Revelation 12:10 describes Satan as the accuser (prosecutor) of the brethren, who accuses them before God day and night. The role of a prosecutor describes our enemy very well. I am not saying that all earthly prosecutors are evil, but they do go into the courtroom with an accusation. Daniel also said that in this courtroom the books were open, didn't he? In any courtroom setting, the prosecutor and the attorney for the defendant will bring with them books or evidence to present to the judge. Daniel 7:22 says that the Ancient of Days (God) made a judgment in favor of the saints. The Judge ruled based on the legal evidence (the books that were opened) in favor of the saints. Well, all of this sounds like a courtroom scene on the earth, but it was actually taking place in the spirit realm of God's throne room.

We need to realize that there are things we can do through our faith in God to change things in the realm of the spirit that will then produce good and lasting change in the natural realm. Someone said that this teaching sounds like it may be a little complex, that learning about how God's spiritual laws function may require more effort. It's true, you may have to do a little more studying, but it will be of great benefit to you and your family to invest more time in God's Word. If a person told you that he does not want to learn about the law of gravity or any other natural laws, what would you say to that? You would probably tell him to make time to learn about them because they may save his life one day. The reason I do not jump off of buildings is because I understand how the law of gravity works. I use the natural laws for my benefit and good don't you? It's time we learn how to use God's spiritual laws and forces for our benefit and good!

If we look at a natural courtroom setting, the presiding judge is the one who decides what the verdict will be for the defendant. If this judge is a man of honesty and integrity, he will only make his decision based on the legal evidence presented to him. If his son is the defendant, he will not allow his emotions to influence his decision. The overall outcome of the court case will be legally based. If the legal evidence is solid enough against the defendant then the judge will have to rule in favor of the plaintiff and the prosecutor. The Bible tells us that it is impossible for God to lie (Numbers 23:19; Hebrews 6:18), and Psalm 89:34 says:

"My covenant I will not break, nor alter the word that has gone out of My lips."

Our Heavenly Father (the Ancient of Days) is the ultimate Judge over all beings and all creation, isn't He? Also, remember that the Word of God is spiritual law, it always works and cannot be broken! When God is presiding in His courtroom concerning a matter, His verdict will always demonstrate His integrity and be executed in full compliance with His spiritual laws; that is why we need to make sure our words and actions agree with His Word. When you and I come to God's throne, according to Hebrews 4:16, we come boldly and confidently because of who we are in Christ. We have a right (experientially) through the Blood of Jesus to come before our Father (who is our Judge) and present our case. Of course it is through our attorney, the Lord Jesus, that we do this. You never have to ask the Lord for permission to come into His courtroom. That is a Divine right and privilege for every Believer.

Also, remember that in the spirit we are already seated in Christ at God's right hand in His throne room or in this case His courtroom. So, we are not actually trying to get into the throne room because we are already there in Christ. Again, when the Bible says to come boldly in, it is talking about us experiencing what has already been done for us through our spiritual position in Christ. When we come in, we come in by faith, we do not come in except by faith, and we do not have to dramatize it and turn it into a great theatrical production. As soon as you open your mouth and start talking to the Lord about whatever the matter is, picture yourself at His throne or in His courtroom presenting your case before Him. Isaiah 43:26 says:

Put Me in remembrance; let us contend together; state your case, that you may be acquitted."

Listen to me now. Our enemy, the devil, is always accusing us before the Judge (God), and it's true that we do not need to know all of his accusations because he is a liar, but if he ever has a legal accusation against us, we need to know what that is. Let me give you an example, God's spiritual law, His

Word, says that by Jesus' stripes we have already been healed. So, that Word is what God honors and watches over to bring to pass in our physical bodies doesn't He? Now, if for the last 10 years you have been confessing that your back will never work right and that you will probably end up in a wheel chair, you are snared by the words of your mouth, you have declared your own guilty sentence even before the Judge has ruled; through your negative confession you have broken God's spiritual law (His Word). You have given the devil a <u>legal right</u> or permission to come into your life and use your authority (which God gave you in Christ) against you; in this case, to give you severe back problems.

The Judge has to rule in favor of the prosecutor (the devil in this case) because He will not pronounce a judgement contrary to His Word (spiritual law). You may say to the Lord, "I love you with all my heart and I am a faithful tither. I don't understand why my back always hurts. I'm your child, why won't you help me?" Even if you say that from the heart of a child speaking to his Father, you still cannot forget that your Father is also your Judge, and He will not break His Word for you, me or anyone else. The reason we can receive healing, prosperity and victory in our lives is not because of our emotions or because we love the Lord a lot, but because of our faith in all that Jesus finished for us at Calvary. Everything we experience comes freely from God's grace through faith. Revelation 19:11 says:

"Now I saw heaven opened, and behold, a white horse. And He who sat on him was called Faithful and True, and in righteousness <u>He judges and makes war.</u>"

This verse is describing the Lord Jesus when he comes back at the Second Advent. Notice the part I underlined. The Lord judges and makes war. Based on the terminology, the words "Judges and war" cause me to mentally picture a courtroom and a battlefield. I can see that before the Lord goes to war or to the battlefield; he makes sure so to speak that everything is legally dealt with in the courtroom. That reminds me that the Lord Jesus only said what He heard the Father say and He only did what He saw the Father do when He walked this earth.

We need to understand as Christians that we also spend time engaged in activities involving a spiritual battlefield or a spiritual courtroom setting, and we need to recognize which setting is the appropriate one to be involved in for the successful outcome we are expecting. If we have been spending years on the battlefield concerning a specific problem or issue and we have not seen any results, that could be a clue that we need to get off the battlefield and visit God's courtroom and talk to the Lord about what's been happening on the battlefield. Other ministers would say that you need to take some time in God's throne room praying and asking Him if you opened up a door to the devil that you are not aware of; if you did, then repent of it in Jesus' Name, renounce any negative words you spoke and head back out to the battlefield.

Based on what I am teaching in this chapter, I might use some different terminology, such as entering the courts of Heaven and asking the Lord if any legal doors have been opened to the devil; but it all means the same thing. When you tell the Lord you are coming into His courts, that does not make him perk up more or become more prone to answer your requests, than if you just said, "I am going to talk to the Lord about this matter." If there is a problem that I need an answer to, it is perfectly normal to say, "I am going to take some time in prayer and discuss this problem with my Father and see if I am missing it somewhere." I do not have to say, "I better take some time and go to the courts of Heaven and talk to the Judge or His Honor about this matter."

There is nothing wrong with using those words, but don't play it up and make it sound like you will not be as spiritually effective unless you use that terminology. I would encourage ministers not to come across sounding spooky or super spiritualizing going into the courts of Heaven as some type of great spiritual event that they are about to participate in. If you are born again, you are God's righteousness in Christ, so just walk right in (spiritually speaking) and start discussing whatever the problem is with your Heavenly Father and expect to hear from Him on how to successfully deal with the issue at hand.

Since Calvary, Christians have been going into

the courts of Heaven and addressing legal matters without calling it the courts of Heaven; not everything about this teaching is brand new revelation that just came out; even though I am glad that God can use different terminology to open up our eyes to spiritual Truth. I like to think of God's throne room as a courtroom because it helps to remind me of the legalities of my redemption.

As I just briefly commented on, a lot of the teaching we have had in the Church has been about the successful implementation of our many spiritual weapons against our enemy on the battlefield. Much of what I teach and have written in my books is on how to release our faith and speak to the mountain, how to resist the devil and run him out of our lives and live in total victory. As Christians, we need to continue declaring these important truths, but we must realize that there is more than just the battlefield out there. If you have been rebuking the devil and confessing you are free from the same problem for 40 years without any manifestation of your miracle or deliverance, then you are probably missing it somewhere. If that has occurred in your life, you need to come off the battlefield (of course spiritually speaking) and spend a little time in God's courtroom.

Because you are already seated in the Heavenly places in Christ, you can enter boldly without fear or condemnation and ask the Lord what is going on. While praying and listening to the Lord, He might give you a word of knowledge about something the devil started through your fourth grandfather back; something the devil meant to continue on as a generational curse. The Holy Spirit may tell you that your alcohol addiction really began about 4 generations before you were born. The Spirit of God may also show you that your fourth past grandfather was heavily involved in witchcraft and other demonic activities which gave Satan legal access into his life so that he became an alcoholic.

Of course, the devil's goal was to see alcoholism spread through him to your third grandfather, second grandfather, first grandfather and to you; also hoping that you will tell your children and grandchildren that they will probably be alcoholics to. Now, any of your past grandfathers could have stopped this in its tracks if they were born again and knew how to enforce their legal rights in Christ. Please remember this: any of them who were not saved, had the law of sin and death working in their lives, thereby giving the devil legal permission to carry on this generational curse of alcoholism in your natural bloodline. You are not going to stop any curse from operating in your life until you become a new man in Christ!

Let's get back now to your present situation. Through all of this revelation about your bloodline, the Lord could then tell you how you gave Satan a legal right to prevent you from experiencing your deliverance from alcoholism. He may show you that you have been playing into the devil's hands through the words of your mouth. You may think and have been told that your confession should be, "I am a recovering alcoholic", but this is not the truth and it disagrees with God's spiritual law (His Word) which teaches you that you are not an alcoholic at all!! Listen! II Corinthians 5:17 says that you are a new man in Christ and <u>all</u> things are brand new. You are not a sinner anymore! The old man is dead and gone; so do not say that you are a recovering sinner, a recovering alcoholic, a recovering sick person or a recovering broke person!!

If you say that you are a recovering alcoholic, you still believe and see yourself as an alcoholic, even though you think you are getting better. You are not an unrighteous sinner in your spirit, but getting better every day! The sinner, sick person, broke person, fear bound person, lustful person and alcoholic you were is gone! That is not you anymore; so quit talking and acting like it is! If you keep talking that way, you are giving the devil legal right to use your authority to keep you bound! Here is how you deal with that situation. First of all, the Bible does not teach that you must repent for the sins of your fourth previous grandfather, those were his sins not yours! What you need to do is repent if you have missed it, and renounce any negative words you have spoken against yourself or anyone else. If you have any unforgiveness in your life, get rid of that immediately and forgive whoever you were holding it against! Once you have done that in faith, and if the Lord doesn't reveal anything else to you, then you are done in the courtroom; it's that simple.

The Courts of Heaven

Please remember that coming into the courts of Heaven and receiving direction from the Lord does not in any way eliminate our responsibility to rebuke and resist the devil. Even though our Heavenly Father is the supreme Judge, he does not resist the devil for us. Under the law, in the old covenant, God rebuked the devour for those who brought their tithes and offerings into the storehouse (Malachi 3:8-10), but in this new covenant under grace, things have changed. Yes, bringing in our tithes and offerings is just as important under grace as it was under the law, but in this new covenant God has told **us** to resist the devil and he will flee from **us** (Matthew 28: 18-20; James 4:7; I Peter 5:8-9). There is not one place in the new covenant which says that God will rebuke the devil for us. For more understanding about this, please see our book "The Prosperous Seed" especially chapter six.

Now, let me repeat something I said about our connection with Adam in chapter three. According to our earthly, natural bloodline and spiritual bloodline, we could say that Adam was our first grandfather; that is, all of humanity came through him. He committed the worst of all sins and brought the worst of all penalties upon every one of us; much, much worse than any of your other grandfathers after Adam. Because of the power of Jesus' Blood shed through His death, we are not only free from the nature of sin and death (the law of sin and death) that Adam brought into this world, we are also forgiven of any sins he committed and we are exonerated from the penalties (the curse of the law) of all of those sins. God's grace was and is more than enough for us!

The Holy Spirit will never tell you that you need to repent for the sins that Adam (your first grandfather) committed, therefore He will not tell you to repent of lesser sins that any of your other grandfathers committed! The Lord Jesus represented you and me, and He took all of our judgement that came upon us through our first grandfather (Adam) and delivered us from it. When that was finished and completed at Calvary, any of the sins committed by any of your past relatives is not on your head! You are not responsible for Adam's sin, so you are definitely not responsible for anybody else's sin in your bloodline after Adam!

I want to share with you some of the Scriptures that ministers use when teaching on generational curses. Generational curses are real, just like the curse of the law is real, but as Believers; we are free and redeemed from them all! Exodus 34:6-7 says:

6. "And the Lord passed before him and proclaimed, "The Lord, the Lord God, merciful and gracious, longsuffering, and abounding in goodness and truth,
7. keeping mercy for thousands, forgiving iniquity and transgression and sin, by no means clearing the guilty, visiting the iniquity of the fathers upon the children and the children's children to the third and fourth generation."

The Lord told Israel that the iniquity of the fathers (referring to the consequences and penalties of their iniquities) would be visited or transferred to their children and as far as the fourth generation. That means their great grandchildren could suffer the consequences of their iniquities. Even though their great grandchildren did not commit the sins they committed, they were still considered guilty. That was really terrible wasn't it? The good news to them was that God would keep mercy for thousands, forgiving iniquity and transgression and sin; but if you chose not to repent and receive forgiveness then you and your future bloodline would be in a bad situation. So, these verses are showing there was a connection made in people's bloodlines. I want us to look now at a story that took place in the book of Joshua concerning the destruction of Jericho. Listen to the warning the Lord gave them about that city.

18. "And you, by all means abstain from the accursed things, lest you become accursed when you take of the accursed things, and make the camp of Israel a curse, and trouble it.
19. But all the silver and gold, and vessels of bronze and iron, are consecrated to the Lord; they shall come into the treasury of the Lord." (Joshua 6:18-19)

The Lord said that if any of them, whether one or more of them, take of the accursed things then all the camp of Israel would be a curse. These were very clear instructions. Now let's see what happened in the beginning of chapter 7.

"But the children of Israel committed a trespass regarding the accursed things, for Achan the son of Carmi, the son of Zabdi, the son of Zerah, of the tribe of Judah, took of the accursed things; so the anger of the Lord burned against the children of Israel." (Joshua 7:1)

According to this verse, God said that all of Israel committed a trespass, even though only one man actually committed the act; his name was Achan. The anger of the Lord burned against all of Israel because of the trespass of one man. During this time in Israel's history, if one person sinned then everyone could suffer the consequences of it; especially if that person's sin was not dealt with appropriately. As you read further into this chapter, you will see that Joshua sent men into a town called Ai to spy out the land. When the men came back, they said that this would be an easy win, and it was not necessary to send very many men into the fight. You probably know the story, when they came against the men of Ai, they were defeated; thirty-six men were struck down.

**6. "Then Joshua tore his clothes, and fell to the earth on his face before the ark of the Lord until evening, he and the elders of Israel; and they put dust on their heads.
7. And Joshua said, "Alas, Lord God, why have You brought this people over the Jordan at all—to deliver us into the hand of the Amorites, to**

destroy us? Oh, that we had been content, and dwelt on the other side of the Jordan!"

10. So the Lord said to Joshua: "Get up! Why do you lie thus on your face?

11. Israel has sinned, and they have also transgressed My covenant which I commanded them. For they have even taken some of the accursed things and have both stolen and deceived; and they have also put it among their own stuff.

12. Therefore the children of Israel could not stand before their enemies, but turned their backs before their enemies, because they have become doomed to destruction. Neither will I be with you anymore, unless you destroy the accursed from among you."

15. Then it shall be that he who is taken with the accursed thing shall be burned with fire, he and all that he has, because he has transgressed the covenant of the Lord, and because he has done a disgraceful thing in Israel." (Joshua 7:6-7, 10-12, 15)

Okay, Israel had an awesome victory at Jericho, but total defeat at Ai. At first, Joshua did not understand how they could do so well then experience such a great loss. Obviously, he was confused and perplexed about the matter. So, he fell on his face and talked to the Lord about it. Based on what I am teaching in this chapter, you could say that Joshua came off the battlefield and went into the courtroom. He knew that they must have missed it somewhere and given the devil a legal entrance into their lives, so he could defeat them. God revealed to Joshua where the door was opened and they dealt with the situation and got it closed. When they went back to Ai they conquered them and had a great victory. At first, Israel suffered because of one man's sin, but after it was corrected, according to God's instructions to Joshua, they all experienced blessings and success.

Let me ask you a question? Where did Joshua receive his instructions on how to fix the problem, on the battlefield or in the courtroom? Yes, it is true that many times while on the battlefield, we just need to be patient and keep praising God until our victory comes to pass, but sometimes we may need to visit the courts of Heaven for some help. Since the courts of Heaven are not a geographical location, but it is God's throne room where we are seated through our union with Jesus, then we can go in and receive whatever help and wisdom we need at the time. Let's be bold to partake of these wonderful sonship rights! Let me share with you one more example of this. II Samuel 21:1 says:

"Now there was a famine in the days of David for three years, year after year; and David inquired of the Lord. And the Lord answered, "It is because of Saul and his bloodthirsty house, because he killed the Gibeonites.""

Remember that David and Israel were in the Abrahamic covenant, and according to that covenant in Deuteronomy chapter twenty-eight, God described the blessings which were available to them. If they hearkened to His voice and obeyed His commandments, the heavens would be opened and they would prosper in all that they do. So, experiencing famine for three years was not part of that blessing, but it was part of the curse operating in their lives. For the curse to operate in their lives, someone had to legally open up a door to the devil and allow him access.

When the Bible says that David inquired of the Lord, it means that he spent some time praying or going into the courts of Heaven to seek an answer. The Lord spoke to him and revealed where the door was opened and who opened it, and then David proceeded to do whatever was necessary to remedy the situation; that is to close off that legal entrance. Please let me remind you again, every time you come into the courts of Heaven, know that through Jesus' blood you can come boldly and with great confidence (Ephesians 3:12)! Come in expecting to hear and receive from the Lord answers to your situation!

Now, I would like to show you something from the Bible that God spoke through the prophet Ezekiel probably seven to eight hundred years after Joshua conquered Jericho. This is a Word that the Lord prophesied through him to Israel while still under the Mosaic laws and hundreds of years before Calvary took place.

1. "The word of the Lord came to me again,

saying,

2. "What do you mean when you use this proverb concerning the land of Israel, saying: 'The fathers have eaten sour grapes, and the children's teeth are set on edge'?

3. "As I live," says the Lord God, "<u>you shall no longer use this proverb in Israel</u>.

4. "Behold, all souls are Mine; the soul of the father as well as the soul of the son is Mine; <u>the soul who sins shall die</u>." (Ezekiel 18:1-4, Emphasis added throughout chapter)

The proverb quoted in verse two is another way of describing what the Lord said in Exodus 34:7 that the consequences of the father's iniquities would be passed on to the third and fourth generation of his children. According to the proverb, if the father ate sour grapes, it would mess up his teeth, but it would also mess up the teeth of his children even though they did not eat the sour grapes. In verse three, the Lord said, "...<u>You shall no longer use this proverb in Israel</u>." In other words, we are not going to do that anymore! Please listen to this! God changed everything through the prophecy of Ezekiel! He said that from now on, I will deal with **each individual** person concerning his or her sins or righteous acts, and the person's children will not be held responsible for what their parents did or didn't do. Wow! I believe that brought a great freedom to the people back then; to know that they (each individual person) were only held accountable for their actions. Let's look at what God said in some more verses in Ezekiel.

5. "But if a man is just and does what is lawful and right;

9. If he has walked in My statutes and kept My judgments faithfully-<u>he is just; he shall surely live</u>!" Says the Lord God.

10. "<u>If he begets a son</u> who is a robber or a shedder of blood, who does any of these things.

13. ...<u>If he has done any of these abominations, he shall surely die; his blood shall be upon him</u>."

14. "<u>If, however, he begets a son</u> who sees all the sins which his father has done, and considers but does not do likewise;

17. Who has withdrawn his hand from the poor and not received usury or increase, but has executed My judgments and walked in My statutes-<u>he shall not die for the iniquity of his father; he shall surely live!</u>

18. As for his father, because he cruelly oppressed, robbed his brother by violence, and did what is not good among his people, behold, <u>he shall die for his iniquity</u>."
(Ezekiel 18:5, 9-10, 13-14, 17-18)

Please let me recap some things here. If you are in Christ, the devil does not have any authority or dominion over you. He does not have a legal right to do anything to you, unless you give him that legal right (Ephesians 4:27).

I John 5:18 says:

"We know that whoever is born of God does

not sin; but he who has been born of God <u>keeps himself</u>, and the wicked one does not touch him."

It is true that God is our Divine protection but we also have a responsibility to guard and keep ourselves by staying full of His Word and walking in all His ways in Christ. If you give place to the devil in your life through doubt, fear and unforgiveness then you are not keeping yourself; so do not get mad at God if you do not experience His goodness and blessings in your life. Even with this always in mind, do not allow the devil to get you into fear by wondering if you have given him place in your life. Never live in fear of your past, much less anyone else's past! Your mind should not be occupied wondering what accusations the devil has been saying about you; that is not keeping yourself. Here is what your mind should be occupied with:

"You will keep him in perfect peace, whose mind is stayed on You, because he trusts in You." (Isaiah 26:3)

"If then you were raised with Christ, seek those things which are above, where Christ is, sitting at the right hand of God.
Set your mind on things above, not on things on the earth." (Colossians 3:1-2)

Something else that I want to remind you of is that if your miracle or healing is taking a long time to be manifested that does not always mean you are giving place to the devil and that you need to have a spiritual court visit. Here are a couple of Scriptures you may have forgotten about:

"If you do not carefully observe all the words of this law that are written in this book, that you may fear this glorious and awesome name, THE LORD YOUR GOD,
then the Lord will bring upon you and your descendants extraordinary plagues-great and <u>prolonged</u> plagues-and serious and <u>prolonged</u> sicknesses." (Deuteronomy 28:58-59)

Part of the curse of the law that the Lord Jesus redeemed us from (Galatians 3:13-14) was <u>prolonged</u> plagues and sicknesses. The slowness of the manifestation of your healing may not be a legal issue that you need to address; it may be a lack of faith and understanding issue. I believe that it would be very wise if you took some time (probably a lot of time) to meditate on Galatians 3:13-14 tied in with Deuteronomy 28. The first 14 verses of Deuteronomy 28 are talking about the blessings and the rest of the chapter describes all of the curses that we are free from.

I do not think most of us have spent much time learning about the curses we are free from. It would greatly benefit you to know the things that you do not have to put up with in your life anymore! You and I are redeemed and free from all sicknesses and diseases of <u>long continuance</u>! Speak to those diseases

The Law of the Spirit of Life in Christ Jesus

and pain, as well as financial debt (and with an attitude like you really expect something to happen), curse the curse that the devil is illegally trying to bring against you and command it all to die and disappear out of your life in the Name of Jesus!! When you do, expect to experience your miracles, and keep expecting and praising God until you do! If after that, you go a long time without seeing and feeling any results, then you may want to spend some time in the courtroom to see if you missed something that you are not aware of.

CHAPTER 5

THE POWER OF RESURRECTION LIFE

When we are talking about the courts of Heaven and confronting legal issues in the bloodlines of Christians, we need to understand that it is not exactly the same as dealing with the legal issues of God's men and women in the Old Testament. So, you have to be especially careful using some Old Testament examples to confirm how the devil may be working in your life today. Our enemy has been totally defeated and we have all authority and dominion over him in Jesus' Name! Before the death and resurrection of Jesus, God's people did not have eternal life, which is spiritual life or the law of the Spirit of life in Christ working in their lives. No matter how many miracles they did or how godly they lived, their spirit was still connected to Satan through the law of sin and death or spiritual death. Their bloodline was corrupted and would stay that way until Jesus came and shed His Blood to redeem us.

Even with all of their blood sacrifices and offerings, they could not declare that they were totally redeemed from the curse of the law because the main part of that curse was the nature or law of sin and death which remained in their spirits until Jesus came and destroyed the power of death. They could partake (by faith in God) of healing, deliverance, prosperity, wisdom, the blessing of Abraham, without being born again. But, eternal life (the law of the Spirit of life in Christ) the very nature of God, they could not experience in their inner man; that was one of the promises they were waiting to experience (Hebrews 11:13). Also, they could not declare that they were the righteousness of God in Christ and that the devil had no place in them.

Remember, when Jesus walked this earth He said, **"...For the ruler of this world is coming, and he has nothing in me."** (John 14:30) When Jesus was here, the law of sin and death did not operate in Him. His bloodline was not corrupted. He was sinless wasn't He? As Christians today, we can declare that in our spirits, in Christ, the devil has no place in us! He does not have any spiritual or legal connection to us. Yes, it is true, we can give place to him in our lives through committing sins and speaking contrary to

God's Word, but that does not sever or destroy our spiritual connection with our Father God! That remains intact and is very strong! We have a clean bloodline as new creations in Christ; so do not let the devil convince you otherwise!

I believe that we need a deeper and greater revelation of how strong the new birth (or eternal life) is in our lives. The new birth is the result of the law of the Spirit of life in Christ setting us free from the law of sin and death. I mentioned in chapter two that it is possible for a Believer to lose his salvation, but it is extremely difficult. It is so important that we understand how powerful God's nature or His life is within us! Every Christian needs to be greatly established in what it means to be a new person in Christ! The devil and his demons cannot overcome or defeat the new man you are! He is afraid of you and me! He is terrified of us! The new creation always avails and prevails (Galatians 6:15)!

Jesus said that He's the way, the truth and the life, and no one comes to the Father except through Him (John 14:6). That means all the other religions in the world that claim they are on the path to God, just by a different way, are totally deceived. They have believed a lie. Anytime you reject Truth, you believe a lie! Jesus not only tells the truth, but He is Truth. Truth is a person. When Jesus stood before Pilate and said, "Everyone who is of the truth hears My voice", Pilate said to Him, "What is truth?" He was looking Truth right in the face and did not even recognize

The Law of the Spirit of Life in Christ Jesus

Him. The Lord said if we are of the truth, we will hear His voice. If you are a Christian, you are of the truth, and you should hear His voice. He said that all life comes from Him, and that life is in us (I John 5:20).

Let us make sure we understand what eternal life is. The most common definition of eternal life that I have heard from Christians and non-Christians is that it means to live forever. But that cannot be correct because only Christians have eternal life. It was a free gift from God. Romans 6:23 says: **"For the wages of sin is death, but the gift of God is eternal life in Christ Jesus our Lord."** When Romans 8:2 talks about the law of the Spirit of life in Christ Jesus, that life is eternal or resurrection life, and the Holy Spirit is the One who imparted that life into our spirits when we were born again. Remember, man is a spirit being, he possesses a soul (mind, will, intellect and emotions) and lives in a body. Man's spirit will never cease to exist. He will exist with God or the devil. One or the other, it is his choice. The Bible teaches that all non-Christians (those who never accept Jesus as their personal Lord and Savior), the devil and all his demons will burn in the lake of fire <u>forever</u>. They will be tormented, but they will live <u>forever</u>; just not with eternal life (Revelation 20:10-15).

Even though the devil and all lost people are alive, it is not with God's life. God's life is called eternal life. The Translator's New Testament published by the British and Foreign Bible Society says:

"Eternal life (Greek-Zoe) in the New Testament is that kind of life which is given to all true believers in Christ. The word 'eternal' draws attention to the <u>quality</u> of that life, not to its duration in a temporal sense. Thus eternal life can be experienced by believers even while subject to the temporal conditions of earthly life. Translators should be careful to avoid expressions which mean no more than a timeless continuation of life after death."

W. E. Vine in his Expository Dictionary of New Testament Words said:

"Eternal life is life as a principle, life in the absolute sense, life as God has it, that which the Father has in Himself, and which He gave to the Incarnate Son to have in Himself, and which the Son manifested in the world." (John 5:26; I John 1:2)

Therefore, the life of God is a spiritual substance. God is a spirit, not flesh (John 4:24). The life of God is what makes God, God. It is His nature, and His nature is now our nature! So when the Spirit of life enters the heart (spirit) of a lost person, He removes sin and death (spiritual) out of his spirit. The nature of Satan is spiritual death, and the Spirit of life in Christ is much greater than the devil's nature of sin and death! The Spirit of life always overcomes spiritual death in the person who believes in the Lord.

Let's take a second and go back to Adam and Eve in the book of Genesis. The Lord said, in chapter 2, verse 17,

"But of the tree of the knowledge of good and evil you shall not eat, for in the day that you eat of it <u>you shall surely die.</u>" We know the story; they died that day, but not physically. God said they would die, and they did, but it was spiritually. In the margin of my Bible, it says that the literal Hebrew for what the Lord said is "In dying you shall die."

Romans 5:12 says:
"Therefore, just as through one man sin entered the world, and death through sin, and thus death spread to all men, because all sinned."

We know that the Apostle Paul was talking about spiritual death spreading to all men because if he was talking about physical death spreading to all men, then everyone on the earth would be dead. There would be no one to save. Jesus couldn't have been born of the Virgin Mary because she would have been dead also. So we know that natural death is not how Adam died that day because he went on to live over 900 years. He did die that day but it was spiritually. Therefore, the question is, "What is spiritual death?" Probably 1000's of preachers have misunderstood this simple truth. I heard someone ask a well-respected and well known TV minister if Jesus died spiritually. He did not even hesitate to think about it. He quickly said, "No, how could God cease to exist." I want you to know that I have great respect for this minister, but that is one of the most ignorant statements I have ever heard. A child could figure this out from the Bible. You don't need a scholar or a theologian's help. Ephesians 2:1 says:

And you He made alive, who were dead in trespasses and sins."

When the Bible says we were dead in trespasses and sins, it is referring to spiritual death, not physical death. Think about this. Before you and I got saved, we were spiritually dead. All of the lost people on this earth are spiritually dead right now; until they receive the new birth or eternal life. Also, the devil and his demons are spiritually dead. Now, if we go by the answer from the T.V. minister, then none of us, including the devil, would exist. Once again, there would be no one for Jesus to die for because no one would exist. W. E. Vine said:

"Death is the opposite of life; it never denotes non-existence. As spiritual life is conscious existence in communion with God, so spiritual death is conscious existence in separation from God."

You might want to read that definition again about ten times! Spiritual death doesn't define whether you exist or not, it defines whom you exist with. It is separation from God. If you are separated from Him, you are automatically connected to the devil. A person who is spiritually dead is still physically alive, or a dead man walking. Even though he is alive, he is not alive in his spirit with "Eternal life". The nature in your spirit identifies who your father is. If you have sin and death in you then your father is Satan (John 8:44). If you have eternal life in you then your father is God. There's not a third choice. Everyone is in one of those two categories.

You can have wonderful social skills, feed the poor and still be a child of the devil. It is not about your highly refined ways of etiquette or your finely educated mind. It is about your spiritual position. **Only** if you have eternal life are you a child of God. As I mentioned earlier in this book, if you have any doubts about salvation, take a moment right now, believe in your heart that Jesus died and arose from the dead. Ask Him to come into your life and confess Him as your Lord. If you will do that and believe what you say, then you will be born again.

A lot of what I am sharing with you about spiritual life and death is even more explained in my book "The Mystery". Understanding these things that we are looking at in this chapter will give you a greater reality of why the law of the Spirit of life in Christ Jesus has set you free from the law of sin and death. I believe that your faith will grow even stronger in living free from everything that has to do with the law of sin and death, and you will become more determined to resist and reject anything that is not part of the law of the Spirit of life in Christ! Reach out with your faith through your confession (Philemon 6) and expect every blessing in the law of the Spirit of life to be manifested in your life!

When God created Adam and Eve, He gave them dominion over all the earth and all creatures. When the devil came to them, they could easily have run him off. They did not have to succumb to his temptation but they chose to yield to their flesh and when their desire was conceived it gave birth to sin, which brought forth spiritual death and later physical death (James 1:14-15). The devil had no connection to man until Adam gave him place and allowed him to connect. In modern day terms, I like to think of it like the internet. The kingdom of darkness is the devil's internet, so to speak. I am just using the internet to illustrate a point here. The only way he could connect with man was through his nature or law of sin and death. He knew if he could replace God's nature in man with his nature then he would have him locked in. But he could not do that just because he wanted to. He had to convince man to use his free will and open up the door to him or give him legal entrance.

Some time ago, I called AT&T because I was having a problem with my computer. The man on the phone asked if he could take over my computer to help me. After I gave him permission, he was controlling my computer. In the same way man gave the devil permission to take over his life "Spiritual computer" and become his "god". Of course in Adam's case he did it through disobeying God's command, or you could say by breaking God's spiritual law in his life. The devil knew he could not override Adam's will and make him do anything, and he cannot make you do anything either! He can only bring a temptation or a suggestion that he hopes you will act on. He hopes that you will disobey God's Word and fall for his lie.

The big problem was not in Adam dying as one individual. If it was only about him, then that would have been over 6000 years ago, and he would just be a history lesson. The problem was, Adam was not alone in his sin (and I am not talking about Eve). He was a representative man, just like our president, congressmen and senators. The decisions they make affect all those they represent, which is everyone in our nation. In Adam's case, he did not represent just one state or nation. He represented the entire human race (I Corinthians 15:21, 22). That meant what Adam got, we got. When he died spiritually, we did to.

It did not matter whether we were there physically when he ate of the fruit. We were in him as our representative. I do not have to be with the president of the United States for his decisions to affect me, because he represents me. Because of Adam, all humanity was lost and separated from God our Creator, and there was not anything we could do about it; that is why Jesus, our wonderful Savior came, to destroy the spiritual link that connected us with the devil and reconnect our spiritual link to God. Here is how He did it.

II Corinthians 5:14 says:
"For the love of Christ compels us, because we judge thus: that if One died for all, <u>then all died</u>."

Hebrews 2:14, 15 say:
"Inasmuch then as the children have partaken of flesh and blood, He Himself likewise shared in the same, that <u>through death</u> He might destroy him who had the power of death, that is, the devil,
and release those who through fear of death were all their lifetime subject to bondage."

Most of the time you will hear Christians say Jesus died to save us, and that is very true. All that He did was to give us life and reconcile or reconnect us with God. But if we just study His death, before we get to the resurrection, you will find that He had to kill us first. I like to say it that way to get people's attention. Did you read closely the end of II Corinthians 5:14? Here's the way most Christians hear that verse in their heads as they read it, "If One died for all, then all were saved". Look at it again. It did not say that did it? Whether you understand it or not, Jesus died so all of us could <u>die</u>. Why? His death was the death of our old man, which was the nature or law of sin and death! The Lord had to pay our penalty for sin. We owed God death. We were supposed to die and go to hell, but Jesus intervened for us. If God in His great mercy had not intervened, we would have stayed separated from Him forever. Jesus came to get us out of our spiritual mess. He knew exactly how to do it. He had to become like we were, and fully represent all of humanity, like Adam did. He knew the only way to make us into new creations was to destroy the old creation. He had to get rid of the old man to make us into the new man. The Way translation says, **"By His death might annihilate the power of him who sways the <u>scepter</u> of deaths terrors."**

A scepter is a ruling staff. Spiritual death or the law of sin and death was the scepter the devil used to rule with. That is what gave him control over the human race. It was the link between him and man, and there was nothing man could do to break it. When Adam sinned, spiritual death entered his spirit. That opened the door for the devil, demons, sin, disease, poverty and all the curse to come into the earth, hence, the devil is referred to as the "god" of this world. Our Father in Heaven knew that the only way He was going to have His family back was to break the devil's link and reestablish His link.

When AT&T took control (set up their link) of my computer, I lost control. No matter what instructions I typed out on my key board, my computer refused to respond. In this case, I temporarily lost my link. Now listen. Before I could have control back, the link between my computer and AT&T had to be broken. It would have proved ineffective for me to ignore the

AT&T link and pretend it did not matter. The only way I would have control back was to remove his control. Once his link was severed, mine was reconnected. God understood this truth before we knew about the internet. He knew the link between man and the devil was in our nature. He so desired to give His nature back to us, but knew that was not possible until our old nature was destroyed and removed. That's why Jesus <u>died</u> for us. John G Lake said,

"Jesus went into the grave not just as a martyr but with Divine boldness. He went into the grave as God's conqueror because He was after something. He went after the power of death and got it. He took it captive and came forth from the grave with the keys of hell and of death!! Triumphant!!"

So, our Lord was not just a martyr. He was on a mission when He went to the cross. He did not sit down until He accomplished all His objectives. Let's go back to the Scripture we looked at that said if One died for all, all died. I believe we need to change our thinking on some things. Here is the way most of the Church thinks of Jesus' death. Picture my wife (Leia) and I standing on the corner of a busy intersection and I step out into oncoming traffic. Without hesitation, my wife quickly steps out and pushes me out of the way. She unselfishly prevents me from being hit but is killed in the process. From that moment on, everyone will say that Leia died to save Dwayne, or she died to <u>prevent</u> me from dying.

That is the way most Christians think of Jesus' death. He died to prevent me from dying. II Corinthians 5:14 did not say if One died for all, then all were prevented from dying. It said the opposite of that didn't it? This is so important for you to get a hold of. Jesus died so we could <u>die</u>. Before we could live with God, we had to die first. What part of us needed to die? Our old man, our unregenerate nature, the nature of sin and death; which was the link to the devil and his curse, to use the same analogy. What Jesus did for us through His death, would have been equal to Him taking us into the street with Him so we could be killed by the oncoming traffic. He so identified Himself with us, in bearing the curse and dying in our place, that God gave us full credit for having died. He died so His death would be the death of our old nature. That is how He broke the link for us.

Now let me tell you how He gave us a new nature and reestablished our link with God. It was when He was quickened or made alive. The Bible says we were made alive together with Him (Ephesians 2:5). We could not experience being made alive until He finished in us what needed to be accomplished through His death. The greater revelation you have of Jesus' death and what that means to you, the greater your revelation will be of His resurrection! Understanding what Jesus did for us at Calvary is the rock of our foundation as a Christian! It is a revelation of Christ! The stronger your faith is developed in this revelation, the less the devil will be able to shake you and lead you astray! Your identity in Christ is crucial to a successful Christian life!!

What I am talking about right now is where the origination and spiritual location of our new bloodline began. So, let me share a few more things with you about His death. Again, in Hebrews 2:14, the word "Destroy" in the Greek means to **render entirely idle, useless, make of no effect and to make void.** This verse says Jesus destroyed "him" who had the power of death. As I have already stated, the devil's power over humanity was through spiritual death (the law of sin and death). When Jesus broke the power of death over us, He broke the power of the devil over us. Satan and death are one. They are connected. To render him useless and ineffective against us is to render death, and all of its consequences, useless and ineffective against us!!

I especially like the definition of the word destroy which means to "**Make void**". I always think of a red void stamped on a check. If I submit a check for $10.00 to the bank and they stamp void on it, my check is then useless, powerless and of no effect. Jesus death was so powerful, it is as though He stamped a red void on Satan's forehead! I like to tell the devil, "Have you looked in the mirror lately? You have been voided out of my life! The power you had over me was destroyed when Jesus killed my old man (nature). The man I was, the man you had dominion

The Law of the Spirit of Life in Christ Jesus

over, is DEAD! You have no more link to me! I have all power and dominion over you in Jesus' Name because of my new connection (nature) with God! The new man I am in Christ now, is totally dead to what my old man was once alive to!" Listen to Hebrew 2:14 in a few other translations:

"...**Render powerless him who rules in the sphere of death, that is, the devil...**" (Hudson)

"...**Through death He might break the power of him who had death at his command...**" (New English Bible)

"...**By His death might annihilate the power of him who sways the scepter of deaths terrors...**" (Way)

"...**In order that by Himself submitting to death He might render powerless him who introduced death into the world...**"
(Stevens)

"...**He might render inoperative...**" (Wuest)
"...**That by [going through] death He might bring to nought and make of no effect him who had the power of death...**" (Amplified)

"...**He took a body himself and became like them; so that by his death he might put an end to him who had the power of death...**" (Basic English)

"...For only as a human being could he die and in dying break the power of the devil who had the power of death..." (The Living Bible)

That is what Jesus did to the devil when He broke the power of death over us. He rendered the devil's power over us: Idle, Useless, Destroyed, Brought to Naught, Ineffective, Void, Powerless, Inoperative and Annihilated!! Still, after saying all of that, some Christians still do not get it. They will say, "I heard what you said, but you do not know how bad my situation is. I feel like all of hell came to my house or is coming against my family. I feel like the devil is screaming in my ears every day." Alright, let us go back to the voided out check. If someone who had the money wrote you a check for $10,000,000, would it not seem like that check was screaming at you? In this case it would be screaming at you in a good way because it is written for so much. Now if the bank stamped a red void on it, would it be any good? I know your answer would quickly be a definite no, but what if I tried to change your mind.

What if I said, "Do you really understand how big that check is? That is a huge amount of money!" Maybe I could get at least $1,000 for it? You would still say no, wouldn't you? Well, we need to respond the same way when dealing with the devil. It does not matter how big he talks or what he tries to do! It does not matter how much he writes against you in the amount of that check! As long as there is a void on that check, it is <u>powerless</u>! Jesus voided out the

The Law of the Spirit of Life in Christ Jesus

devil's power over us at Calvary for eternity! It does not matter how big the check is he writes against us! It is useless and ineffective in our lives! Believe that! Declare that! Stand on that from now on! Do not just try it for two weeks! Make it your way of life and you will start seeing results!

In this chapter I have been talking about what was happening behind the scenes so that the law of the Spirit of life could make us free from the law of sin and death. Therefore, I think it is important to remind you not to forget about God's spiritual forces which operate in His Kingdom and in our lives. These spiritual forces are the reason God's spiritual laws operate as laws. If we look at the natural law of gravity again, we will see that the law of gravity is a law because of the force of gravity on this earth. The reason that man came to the conclusion that what goes up must come down is because of the invisible force of gravity. As I said before, a law is something that always works, unless a higher law overrides it. Since the force of gravity guarantees that everything has to come down once it is released into the air, it is considered a law.

Now, let us go back to our understanding of how God's Kingdom functions. In Galatians chapter five, the Apostle Paul talks about the works of the flesh as well as the fruit of the spirit. I believe it will help you when studying the fruit of the spirit to understand that it is not the fruit of the Holy Spirit. It is the fruit of your reborn spirit by the Holy Spirit. The Spirit of

God is not bearing the fruit; He is producing it through you. The life and ability to bear the fruit comes from Him, but the fruit is on the branches and not on the vine (John 15:1-8).

Galatians 5:22, 23 say:
"But the fruit of the Spirit is love, joy, peace, longsuffering, kindness, goodness, faithfulness,
gentleness, self-control. <u>Against such there is no law</u>." (Emphasis added throughout chapter)

We need to realize that these are not just emotional feelings, but powerful spiritual forces. No demonic force can stop the force of love from working, and God is love. No one can defeat Him! Think about light for a minute. When the light comes on in a room, darkness flees. There is nothing it can do to override the light. God is light! Light always wins, just as love always wins! I believe God wants us to understand that there are no other laws that can stop these spiritual forces from working. Why is that important? It is these spiritual forces and others that set the law of the Spirit of life in Christ into operation in our lives. When you believe and confess that the law of the Spirit of life has made your body free from the law of sin and death (which includes all diseases), the force of your faith in God sets that law in motion to bring to pass your healing! When you experience your healing, you are experiencing the law of the Spirit of life in Christ being manifested in your mortal body. It works the same way for your finances and in every area of your life.

The Law of the Spirit of Life in Christ Jesus

When he said, in Galatians 5:23, **"Against such there is no law,"** I believe that he was saying that there is no demonic law, natural law or man-made law that can stop these spiritual forces from working. Also, when it comes to the Jewish laws, they cannot produce these fruits of the spirit in man because they are fruit or forces that come out of the born again spirit. The Jewish laws cannot produce the fruit of the new nature because they cannot give man a new nature. Obeying the Jewish laws cannot change man's nature or cleanse his conscience (Hebrews 9:13-14); only the Blood of Jesus through His death and resurrection can do that. So, only new men and women in Christ can bear the fruit of the spirit and release these awesome spiritual forces! Look at what Proverbs 4:23 says:

"Keep your heart with all diligence, for out of it spring the <u>issues</u> of life."

Out of your heart, or for a Christian, out of your reborn spirit spring the issues of life. I believe that the Lord is talking about the fruit of the spirit or these spiritual forces coming up from your spirit and being released into your life. These issues of life are the spiritual forces that set the law of the Spirit of life into operation to destroy every effect of the law of sin and death.

In Galatians 5:19-21, Paul describes some of the works of the flesh. He also says that those who <u>practice</u> such things will not inherit the kingdom of

God. The works of the flesh result in demonic spiritual forces being set in motion which open the door for the law of sin and death to work in a person life; whether Christian or non-Christian. Just because you have been born again does not mean the law of the Spirit of life will be automatically demonstrated in every area of your life. Again, everything with God works and is received by faith.

Notice that Paul used the word "practice" like the Apostle John did as we discussed in the first chapter. In the Greek, the word "practice" refers to sinning habitually. Christians can sin and make mistakes, but continually living day after day in unrepentant sin, like they did when they were lost, would cause one to question their salvation. Only the Lord truly knows people's hearts. But if that person has rejected Jesus as his Lord then the law of sin and death is operating in his life, resulting in spiritual death. Remember, as we have already talked about, the law of sin and death came into man through Adam's sin. Man (by his own efforts) could not remove it. Only Jesus could, through His sacrifice for us.

Romans 8:3, 4 say:
"For what the law could not do in that is was weak through the flesh, God did by sending His own Son in the likeness of sinful flesh, on account of sin: He condemned sin in the flesh,
That the righteous requirement of the law might be fulfilled in us who do not walk according to the flesh but according to the Spirit."

The Law of the Spirit of Life in Christ Jesus

I think some confusion has come to Christians concerning the word "flesh". It can refer to the physical body or symbolically to the sin nature (spiritual death, the old man). There is also a type of connection between man's spirit, mind and body. Don't forget what we discussed about Satan's spiritual link to man. The reason we could not use our body (flesh) to fulfill the righteous requirements of the law was because of the spiritual link (sin nature or flesh) that connected us to the devil. He had an open door or avenue through our spirits to manipulate our bodies to commit sin. Romans 6:6 says that when our old man (spiritual nature) was crucified, our bodies (flesh) were rendered inoperative to produce sin, showing a connection between man's spirit and his body. That does not mean we cannot sin, but it means we don't have to. We now have dominion over sin!

No matter how much we tried to walk after the spirit and use our minds and bodies to live a holy life, we would always end up failing, as long as we had the law of sin and death in our spirits. We were like puppets to the devil. He pulled the strings. Now, when the law of the Spirit of life came in and set us free, that severed our ties with the kingdom of darkness! When our ties were severed, our minds and fleshly bodies were free to have a new master, the Lord Jesus Christ. As I said in chapter one, to walk after the spirit is to walk from the inside out. We are now capable of doing that, and it will produce holiness and the fruit of the spirit in our lives; all because the law of the Spirit of life in Christ Jesus has made us free from the law of sin and death!! Maybe Galatians 5:24, 25 will make more sense now.

**"And those who are Christ's have crucified the flesh with its passions and desires.
If we live in the Spirit, let us also walk in the Spirit."**

The phrase "Have crucified" is in the past tense. Referring to something already finished. We know our "physical" flesh needs to be crucified every day; that is, any ungodly desires. So what is Paul talking about here? He is talking about the other meaning for the word "Flesh"; the old man, sin nature or law of sin and death. That man has already been crucified, killed and buried with Christ. Your old self is dead and gone! Lost people cannot live in the spirit. To live in the spirit means you are born again (Romans 8:8-9). To walk in the spirit, has to do with your physical body. That is something we learn to do better each day. It is what the Lord meant at the end of verse 4 in Romans, chapter 6.

"Therefore we were buried with Him through baptism into death, that just as Christ was raised from the dead by the glory of the Father, <u>even so we also should walk in newness of life</u>."

Walking in newness of life is walking in the spirit. The glory of the Father is the Holy Spirit or the Spirit of life (Romans 8:11). He is the One who made us alive spiritually, but He also makes our bodies alive with perfect health. John G Lake was talking about that in his testimony, wasn't he? The law of the Spirit of life in Christ is not just for the new birth, so we can go to Heaven. It can be manifested in our minds, bodies, finances and every area of our lives. But we have to believe and expect it to!

The Lord wants us to learn to flow so well in the law of the Spirit of life in Christ that the law of sin and death can never operate in our lives again. My body is healed because I am free from the law of sin and death. The reason that is true is because all sickness and disease is under that law. Since I'm free from that law which gives the curse its power, then I am free from the curse. I live by a higher law now, so I can expect to live free from all sickness and disease. That's why I confess, "If any sickness touches my body it will instantly die in Jesus' Name because the law of the Spirit of life in Christ has made me free from the law of sin and death!"

When I think about walking in the spirit or in the law of the Spirit of life in Christ, I like to think of a man in an enclosed snow plow in the middle of a winter blizzard. There may be snow everywhere, solid white to the north, south, east and west. In my mind, I imagine the snow as the law of sin and death; that is, the curse which is covering this world. As the snow plow travels down the road, it does not matter how deep the snow is or how close it may be to the man in the plow, because it cannot touch him! The plow, and not the man, shoves the snow out of the way! There is nothing the snow can do to get to the man, as long as he stays in the plow! I like to picture the law of the Spirit of life in Christ Jesus as the plow shoving all sin, poverty, sickness, depression, fear and demons out of my way as I walk down the road of life! I believe that is what is happening for me every day as I walk and live in Christ (Colossians 2:6-7)! I hope that you believe the same way!

A word of warning! Don't think that once you set the law of the Spirit of life into motion it will continue to work for you perpetually, no matter how you live. Everything about God is connected to faith, love, forgiveness and holiness. As long as you stay in faith and live for God this law will always work for you. John G Lake operated in this law so well, when the bubonic plague touched him it died instantly! Guess what? His success in functioning in God's life and power did not eliminate the law of sin and death in the world around him. Other people were still dying. They did not know how to override the law of sin and death like he did. They did not know how to live free from that law. That did not mean they were bad people. I do not know how to set the laws of aerodynamics into motion and fly a plane, but that does not mean I am a bad person. It just means I am ignorant of those natural laws.

The Lord said in Hosea 4:6, **"My people are destroyed for lack of knowledge..."** I may not know a lot about how everything works in this world. I am not trying to be an expert in everything, that is not my goal in life. The knowledge that I am thirsty and hungry for is to know Jesus and the power of His resurrection! How about you? Spiritually speaking, I want to get my PHD (maybe 3 or 4 of them) in who I am in Christ and who He is in me!! Don't you? Let's follow Paul's example in Philippians 3:13, 14.

"Brethren, I do not count myself to have apprehended; but one thing I do, <u>forgetting</u> those things which are behind and reaching forward to those things which are ahead.
I <u>press</u> toward the goal for the prize of the upward call of God in Christ Jesus." AMEN!!

CHAPTER 6

DUAL CITIZENSHIP

In the United States of America, of which I am a citizen, there is always talk on the news about people's rights. When it comes to the rights of American citizens, they expect to experience every benefit and privilege available to them. Many Americans are very well versed in their legal rights, and they do not like it one bit when someone or some organization tries to take away those rights. As Believers, we need to become just as well versed, if not more, in our Christian bill of rights! I do not think that most Christians realize that they also have a dual citizenship. They not only have a natural one but also a spiritual one, and within their spiritual citizenship are many wonderful legal rights and privileges. As an American, I am a citizen of the United States. As a

Christian, I am a citizen of Heaven.

"Now, therefore, you are no longer strangers and foreigners, but fellow citizens with the saints and members of the household of God." (Ephesians 2:19)

The old man we used to be in Adam was not a citizen in God's Kingdom and household because he had the wrong nature. One has to be a new man (referring to male or female) in Christ to become a citizen. Why? Because only the new man has a new nature. To become a citizen in the household of God, you must be born again or spiritually birthed into God's Kingdom. You must receive a new nature! I became a citizen of this nation by being born here; my citizenship came through my birth into the United States. There are also people, who became citizens by other means, but there is only one way to become a citizen of Heaven, and that is through the new birth or receiving a new nature within.

Your nature in your spirit identifies the spiritual state and place you have been born into. When Adam and Eve died spiritually, they moved to a different state or place. They moved from God's Kingdom into the devil's kingdom. They moved from God's household of righteousness to Satan's den of iniquity. So, your spiritual nature determines who your citizenship is with; which will determine what kind of rights you have or don't have. In the dictionary, the word "Citizen" means **a legally recognized subject**

Dual Citizenship

of a state or commonwealth. I want to remind you again as we talk about citizenship that everything in the spirit realm is legally based. Our natural citizenship is recognized and based on the laws governing the country we live in.

We are citizens of Heaven because Jesus legally destroyed that nature (law) of sin and death (which made us citizens of hell) and replaced it with the law of the Spirit of life in Christ; which gave us automatic citizenship in the household of God. Again, that automatic citizenship came when we received a new nature. Everything the Lord did for us was legally accomplished wasn't it? The greater reality you have of all that Jesus legally finished for you at Calvary, the greater reality you will have of all your rights and privileges as a Believer!

Here is another reason for understanding the importance of having a new nature and knowing that the old one is dead and removed out of your spirit. I have heard preachers say that Christians have two natures within them, and here is how you recognize the two natures. When they get up in the morning and are mean throughout the day that is the result of the old nature of sin and death rising up. On the other side of the picture, I heard them say that when you are loving and nice, that is the new nature gaining the ascendancy. If that explanation was true then every Christian would be spiritually schizophrenic. Listen very closely here! You may be able to have dual citizenship within two different earthly nations, you

The Law of the Spirit of Life in Christ Jesus

can be a citizen on the earth and in Heaven, but you cannot be a citizen of Heaven and hell at the same time! You can only have one nature in your spirit, and that nature determines which kingdom you have been born into. Your spiritual nature determines where your citizenship lies.

That is why I took time in the last chapter explaining in detail why the death of Jesus was so important, and I want to share with you something else about that in this chapter, because it ties into why we are citizens in God's household. As I said before, Jesus' death was the death of our old man (old nature)! Do you understand now that the Lord Jesus had to die and arise from the dead? There was not anything He could do to redeem us without dying. Our old nature had to be exterminated and eliminated so that God could give us a new nature and make us into new creations! I want to say something else to add to that, and it will probably shake up your thinking a little bit. When Jesus came to this earth He had to do more than just shed His Blood. Our Lord shed His Blood in the Garden. didn't He? But after doing that, He did not tell everyone that they were redeemed, and then preceded on to Heaven. He was in such agony while praying that His sweat became like great drops of Blood falling down to the ground (Luke 22:44); but after this happened He went on to suffer much, much more. Did you know that you do not have to die to shed your blood; you can do that shaving can't you?

If all that the Lord had to do was to shed His Blood, then God allowed Him to go through a lot of unnecessary sufferings ranging from the 39 stripes, nailed to the cross and the sufferings in hell. Again, if you think about it, Jesus could have stood up on a big rock after gathering a group of people around him, taken a knife, cut His wrist (which is the shedding of blood) and told all the people watching that He was, at that very moment, obtaining eternal redemption for them. Even though He could have done that, you know as well as I do that He still had to die on the cross and arise from the dead. Even though you know that is true, do you understand why?

Think about the example of all of the old covenant sacrifices. Weren't they all types and shadows of Jesus' ultimate sacrifice for us? How was the blood obtained from the animals for the sacrifices? Did they have one lamb that they would use for each sacrifice? So, every time they needed to offer blood, they would take a knife and cut the lamb's leg and get some blood, then put a band aid on it until the next sacrifice? No, they did not need any band aids. The animal sacrifice died with the shedding of its blood. Again, the animal did not need to die if all they needed was some blood; yet it gave its blood through death, well so did the Lamb of God. Hebrews 9:22 says:

"And according to the law almost all things are purified with blood, and without shedding of blood there is no remission."

The Law of the Spirit of Life in Christ Jesus

This verse said that "Almost all things" are purified with blood. Does that mean there was something that animal blood could not purify? The blood of animals could not cleanse man's conscious and give him a new nature; only the Blood of Jesus could do that through His death. Jesus washed all of our sins away and keeps us cleansed everyday through His precious Blood; and through His death, He destroyed him who had the power of death.

Look at Hebrews 9:16-17,
"For where there is a testament, there must also of necessity be the death of the testator,
For a testament is in force after men are dead, since it has no power at all while the testator lives."

Remember, the Bible is divided into the Old and New Testaments, or the old and new covenants. A testament is a will which explains what money or goods are being left to someone else after the testator (the one who wrote the will) dies. In other words, the will does not go into operation until there is a death; in this case the death of the testator. If the testator sheds his blood that does not cause the will to go into effect, there has to be a death. Let me give you another Scripture that I have used before.

"And if Christ is not <u>risen</u>, your faith is futile; you are still in your sins!" (I Corinthians 15:17 Emphasis added throughout chapter)

The Holy Spirit said that our faith is futile or

Dual Citizenship

useless if Jesus did not rise from the dead; putting great emphasis on His resurrection (please see our book "Resurrection Witnesses" for more teaching on the importance of Jesus' resurrection). He did not say that our faith is futile if Jesus did not shed His Blood or die. What does that mean? It means that our Lord had to shed His Blood, be crucified, die, be buried, be made alive, conquer all of hell, arise from the dead, ascend into Heaven and sit down at God's right hand to complete our redemption. That is why we are now citizens in the household of God.

So, our Christian rights and freedoms came to us through our spiritual birth; not through our education, race, culture or financial status. What I have been teaching in this book describes the history and foundation of our new bloodline in Christ. Leviticus 17:11 tells us that the life of the flesh is in the blood. Well, the resurrection life of Jesus is in His Blood and has totally cleansed us; that is the life (or the law of the Spirit of life in Christ) flowing through our spiritual veins and working mightily in every part of our lives! Let me show you an earthly example about citizenship using the Apostle Paul.

"And as they bound him with thongs, Paul said to the centurion who stood by, "Is it lawful for you to scourge a man who is a Roman, and uncondemned?"

When the centurion heard that, he went and told the commander, saying, "Take care what you do, for this man is a Roman."

Then the commander came and said to him," Tell me, are you a Roman?" He said, "Yes."

The commander answered, "With a large sum I obtained this citizenship." And Paul said," But I was born a citizen."

Then immediately those who were about to examine him withdrew from him; and the commander was also afraid after he found out that he was a Roman, and because he had bound him." (Acts 22:25-30)

Naturally speaking, Paul knew that he was a Roman citizen. He knew therefore that he had certain rights didn't he? But, if he had not brought up those rights to the commander, he would not have enjoyed those privileges. When a person comes over to our country and becomes a citizen, he starts learning about the laws of the land and what rights have been bestowed upon him. As citizens of Heaven, we need to do the same thing. We need to believe and confess our rights! Paul did that concerning his rights as a Roman, but he also told us to do that concerning our rights as a Christian.

"That the sharing of your faith may become effective by the acknowledgement of every good thing which is in you in Christ Jesus." (Philemon 1:6)

We do not confess the Word of God just to have something positive to say, but to proclaim what our Father in Heaven has done for us. When you start believing what you are declaring, you can expect to experience it! Look what Jesus said about the woman who was bent over with a spirit of infirmity.

**11. "And behold, there was a woman who had a spirit of infirmity eighteen years, and was bent over and could in no way raise herself up.
12. But when Jesus saw her, He called her to Him and said to her, "Woman, you are loosed from your infirmity."
13. And He laid His hands on her, and immediately she was made straight, and glorified God.
16. So ought not this woman, being a daughter of Abraham, whom Satan has bound-think of it-for eighteen years, be loosed from this bond on the Sabbath?"** (Luke 13:11-13, 16)

This woman was not born again yet, and was living in the old covenant; but she had rights with God, didn't she? The Lord said that she had a right to be free from that bondage of disease. The devil had her bound. The devil will always try to steal your rights from you but notice what happened in this story. King Jesus and the spiritual government of God recognized her rights. Through her covenantal relationship with God, she had a right to be free. The devil was illegally binding her and the Lord Jesus recognized that when He told her to be <u>loosed</u> from her infirmity.

In the Greek language, the word "Loosed" means

to **relieve, release, dismiss and pardon**. According to the dictionary, it means **a remission of the legal consequences of an offence.** These two definitions sound a lot like legal or courtroom terms. You could say that the devil had her bound through the law of sin and death, but Jesus came along and set a higher law into motion. Remember, the devil can only attack you by using his governmental or kingdom laws; he cannot use God's spiritual laws. The spiritual laws of God only belong to the citizens of God's household. Jesus, through His declaration or prophetic Word to her, superseded what Satan set in motion and the woman was instantly healed!

Let me give you some more (good) legal terminology from the Bible. Matthew 16:19 says:

"And I will give you the keys of the kingdom of heaven, and whatever you bind on earth will be bound in heaven, and whatever you loose on earth will be loosed in heaven."

Keys in the Bible represent authority. If you have the keys to a building, then you have the legal right to enter that building. Through the law of the Spirit of life we can bind up anything the devil tries to do, and we can loose or set free anything or anyone he has bound. He cannot bind what we loose and he cannot loose what we bind! He does not have a legal right to; therefore, he does not have the authority! As God's citizens, we have the authority and legal right in Jesus' Name to allow on this earth what is allowed

Dual Citizenship

in Heaven. We also have the authority to forbid from operating on this earth what is forbidden from operating in Heaven. Look with me now at Matthew 8:7-9. A centurion came to Jesus wanting Him to heal his servant whom he left at home.

7. "And Jesus said to him, "I will come and heal him."
8. The centurion answered and said, "Lord, I am not worthy that You should come under my roof, but only speak a word, and my servant will be healed.
9. For I also am a man under authority, having soldiers under me, and I say to this one, 'Go,' and he goes; and to another, 'Come,' and he comes; and to my servant, 'Do this,' and he does it."

The Lord told him that he had great faith and to go his way and that as he had believed, it would be done for him. His servant was healed that same hour. This man understood where his authority came from as a soldier. He knew that it was based upon the laws governing the Roman military structure. It was by this knowledge and his experience that this centurion understood why Jesus had to be operating by some type of legally based system; that is why he recognized Jesus' authority. Once again, I am not talking about the Jewish laws, but the spiritual laws of God's Kingdom. Because we are in Christ, the Lord has given us authority to execute His spiritual laws.

The Law of the Spirit of Life in Christ Jesus

The centurion probably heard testimonies about Jesus, how that He just spoke a word and demons, disease and the weather obeyed Him. This soldier understood the basis of that kind of authority. The Lord said that he had great faith didn't He? Therefore, our faith in God has a very important connection to our authority as a Believer. So, our Lord was very proficient in releasing His faith for the function and operation of God's spiritual laws. He knew how to experience the full benefits of His rights. We need to be just as proficient; because Jesus told us (John 14:12-14) that we can do the same works (miracles, healings...) He did and greater works in His Name. That requires using our faith to release the law of the Spirit of life in Christ into the people we are ministering to; so, they can be free from the law of sin and death!

In my book "In Christ" I have a chapter about the secret place described in Psalm 91, and I emphasize the point that our secret place is in Christ Jesus. He is our true secret place. In saying that, I want to share with you some more Scriptures which have to do with our legal rights of Divine protection. Isaiah 54:14 & 17 say:

"In righteousness you shall be established; you shall be far from oppression, for you shall not fear; and from terror, for it shall not come near you.
No weapon formed against you shall prosper, and every tongue which rises against you in judgment you shall condemn. This is the heritage

of the servants of the Lord, and their righteousness if from Me, says the Lord."

Psalm 31:20 says:
"You shall hide them in the secret place of Your presence from the plots of man; You shall keep them secretly in a pavilion from the strife of tongues."

The New Living Translation says, **"...You shelter them in your presence, far from accusing tongues."**

The Message Bible says, **"...You silence the poisonous gossip."**

In Christ, our secret place, God protects us from the strife of tongues. The Lord guards and protects us from any negative and illegal words spoken against us. He said that we will condemn (renounce, rebuke and render powerless) every tongue (word) that rises up against us in judgment. Again, the word judgment sounds like a legal term. Listen to this. The Hebrew word for "Strife" means: **adversary, controversy, to contest personal or legal.** In the dictionary, the word "Contest" means: **to oppose, take a stand against, challenge, call into question.** All of these words strongly imply courtroom activity; things that we can legally and successfully deal with in the courts of Heaven.

Like God's spiritual law (the Bible) says, we can

contest any words of judgment spoken against us. We have the authority and a legal right to declare those words ineffective! That means no one can put a curse on us! No one can speak anything evil over our lives that will hurt us! Let me say it this way. We cannot stop people from using their mouths and speaking evil against us; but whatever they say, we can destroy with our faith filled words! I am not talking about hurting the people but destroying their ungodly and fear filled words. They are attacking us by their words through the law of sin and death, but we can always overcome and destroy their words through the law of the Spirit of life in Christ Jesus! We have the legal right to render powerless any words spoken against us!

Also, on the other side of this, you may be in God's courtroom discussing a matter with Him, and He reveals to you words which you spoke contrary to His Word (spiritual law). You can then repent for speaking those words and at the same time render and declare them powerless against you in Jesus' Name! Isn't wonderful to be a citizen in the household of God? We have so many great benefits and privileges that we are still learning about! Get your Bible out and study it every day! If you think about it, the United States has a constitution which explains how this nation is to be governed, in like manner, the Kingdom of God has a constitution which explains how it functions and is to be governed; it is called the Bible. The Bible is our Heavenly constitution.

CHAPTER 7

THE ANCIENT OF DAYS

There is no other god besides our God! The prophet Daniel referred to Him as the Ancient of Days. He is our Heavenly Father and the supreme Judge over everything and everyone. Isaiah 43:11 & 13 say:

11. "I, even I, am the Lord, and besides Me there is no savior.
13. Indeed before the day was, I am He; and there is no one who can deliver out of My hand; I work, and who will reverse it?"

"Thus says the Lord, the King of Israel, and his Redeemer, the Lord of hosts: I am the First and I am the Last; besides Me there is no God."

The Law of the Spirit of Life in Christ Jesus

(Isaiah 44:6)

In Isaiah 43:13, the prophet describes God as before the day was, which is referring to His title, the Ancient of Days, He existed before time began. He is eternal. He always was, is and will always be. Daniel saw Him as with a white garment on, the hair of His head was like pure wool and His throne was a fiery flame (Daniel 7:9-10). Also, Hebrews 12:29 says, **"For our God is a consuming fire."** In the Bible, the word "Fire" is symbolic for cleansing and judgment. In Daniel's vision, he saw the Lord sitting as Judge in a courtroom setting.

When God put man on this earth everything was good, but Adam sinned and the curse came into this world. As the Judge of mankind, God made it very clear, in the beginning, when dealing with His people, that they only had two choices in life. They could enjoy the blessings of Heaven or live their lives consumed with the curse. Here is what the Lord said:

"I call heaven and earth as witnesses today against you, that I have set before you life and death, blessing and cursing; therefore choose life, that both you and your descendants may live." (Deuteronomy 30:19)

God made it very clear that we have a choice. He did not say that the choice was His. He said that the choice was ours. Sometimes I hear people say that God is sovereign, meaning He can do anything He

The Ancient of Days

wants to in our lives, and that whatever happens to us is God's will. Well, the verse we just read in Deuteronomy 30:19 belies that statement; it proves it to be a lie. The Lord made it very clear that what happens to us is based on the choices we make; not on the choices He makes for us.

In the dictionary, the word "Sovereign" means possessing supreme or ultimate power; and that is very true for our Heavenly Father (Judge over all creation). Some people think that because God has unlimited power, He can do anything. He can as long as it does not go against His nature and character. If you think about it (from God's Word), He cannot lie, He cannot tempt anyone with evil, He cannot change and He cannot do anything bad. He always uses His power for good, but here is something you may not have thought about, when God destroys evil, that is good. God is the best of all fathers isn't He? He will always protect His children from evil, wicked men and women; and remember, that is always good.

Listen, when it comes to me, I only want to do well to others. I only want to be a blessing to people, but if you try to hurt my wife or children, then I am going to defend them; my coming to their defense will demonstrate my goodness to them, as well as others who may be watching. Now, I will be glad to pray for God to heal you after I stop you from hurting my family, but I will not stand by and watch you do something that would endanger their lives! So, getting back to our choices in life; if you want life, you have to choose it. Well, how do you do that? He told us how in Proverbs 18:21, when He said that life and death, or you could say blessing and cursing, are in the power of the tongue. The way we choose which one we want is by the words of our mouths, and it is by the words of our mouths that we release our faith to activate spiritual laws. I said all of that to say this, any bad things you have experienced or are experiencing in your life are not from God, and He did not have anything to do with it!

Someone else said, "You know that God has a purpose for everything that happens to you." No He doesn't! The Bible does not say that! The people who say that are those who do not want to accept responsibility for their words and actions; they want to blame God or somebody else for their problems and why their lives are a wreck. The same people will say, "There is a reason for everything or God must have a reason for this mess I am going through." Whenever they say there is a reason for everything, they are implying that the Lord had something to do with them being broke, sick, divorced, losing a child or having a car wreck; but God had absolutely nothing to do with those things! The main reason for the bad things which have happened in your life and mine in the past was from our own stupidity, ignorance and unbelief. Every good thing we have experienced was from our loving Father.

We need to understand just what our Heavenly Father (our Judge) does and does not do. I John 4:8

says that God is love. He does not just have love, He is love. James 1:13-14 say:

13. "Let no one say when he is tempted, "I am tempted by God"; for God cannot be tempted by evil, nor does He Himself tempt anyone.

14. "But each one is tempted when he is drawn away by his own desires and enticed."

James 1:17 says:
"Every good gift and every perfect gift is from above, and comes down from the Father of lights, with whom there is no variation or shadow of turning."

Therefore, only good things come from God. Someone had the audacity to say, "Maybe that disease was actually something good and I just did not know it." If that person really believes that then he is stupid. If you think that the cancer eating up that person's body or the person starving to death through financial poverty is God's will then you are really deceived by the devil, and your thinking is very warped. You must always remember that God cannot temp anyone with evil! There is not any evil in Heaven; only good. There is perfect health, life, righteousness, wealth, joy, peace and total victory in Heaven; and Jesus said for us to pray for God's will in Heaven to be done on the earth. Any time you read a verse in the Bible that sounds like the Lord is speaking contrary to His will in Heaven being done on the earth, then you know that you have misinterpreted that verse. If you have not learned this then please learn it now; God will never say or do anything contrary to His Word because His Word is His will to us. The Lord will never break His Word!

There are Christians who have been taught that the Lord does not send bad things or do bad things, but He does allow it. We need to clarify what we mean when we say that God allows bad things to happen, because most of the time when people say that, they are still implying that He had something to do with it. They are describing God almost like a mafia boss. The mafia boss did not actually murder the man but he did allow and probably paid for someone else to do it. It is true that the Lord does allow things to happen but not the way most people use that word. When God allows something, it simply means that He did not stop it from happening.

As you know, stealing is wrong, but as a Christian, if you decide to rob a bank, God will allow you to do it; in other words, if you will not listen to any of His promptings to resist doing that, and if you insist on robbing that bank anyway, then God will not stop you. So, after you have robbed the bank, do not turn around and say, "I do not know why God allowed me to rob that bank." He had nothing to do with it! He will never override our wills. We can do anything we choose to do. God will not make us go to church or read our Bibles. He will let you and I make all kinds of mistakes in life if we choose not to listen to his instructions and guidance.

In Deuteronomy 28, the Lord told the children of Israel that if they disobeyed His commandments, curses would come upon them, and just like the Lord said, whenever they disobeyed, the curses came on them. If they complained and said, "We do not understand why God allowed these curses in our lives," they would be implying that He must have had something to do with it, or there was a higher reason, which they did not understand, for their sufferings. The truth is, God had nothing to do with it, He told them what choices to make to prevent the curses from coming on them, but they chose not to obey Him.

I have notice over and over again, that many Christians like to come up with a "Spiritual" reason for their irresponsibility's and mistakes; so that it does not sound like they missed God or messed up. They do not want anyone to think that they are not spiritual. They never want to point the guilty finger at themselves; only at someone else. They want to satisfy their consciences by believing that their (probably a lack of faith) mistakes serve some type of greater purpose in the Divine plan of God for their lives. They will say, "I don't know why that person died so young, I don't know why that person is crippled or why he lost his job. We just don't understand these things. I do know that God did not do it, but He did allow it, and we will probably never know the reason why until we get to Heaven."

The Law of the Spirit of Life in Christ Jesus

They want to believe that all things, whether good or bad, are in God's "Mysterious" Divine plan. You know what? The devil loves it when Christians believe that way, because if they think that God is involved in the bad things happening to them, then they will not use their faith and authority as a Believer to resist it. Ignorantly and unknowingly they will allow the devil to have his way in their lives, thinking they are glorifying God in the pain and suffering inflicted upon them. I think that some of this misunderstanding, stems from the way our English version of the Bible was written.

About 44 years ago when I first started studying the Word of God, I learned that through the books I read, by Bible theologians, ministers and scholars, that the Old Testament was written in Hebrew, but in the English language there are not any permissive verbs. For example, in Deuteronomy 28:20, it starts off by saying, "The Lord will send on you cursing, confusion, and rebuke..." In that same chapter, verse 24 says, "The Lord will change the rain of your land to powder and dust..." Also, in verse 27, "The Lord will strike you with the boils of Egypt..." Based on the way those verses were translated in our English Bibles, it sounds like God was doing all those bad things. If we do not have a permissive verb in our English language, then you can understand why they translated those verses in the causative sense.

Once again, when verses like that (in the Old Testament) were translated into English, they were translated in the causative sense, so that it sounds like God was the source of the people's problems. Always remember, the correct way to interpret God's Word is with His Word. Your understanding of a Scripture must agree with the rest of the Scriptures. As I brought out already, the Bible says that God is perfect love and He is all good and cannot tempt anyone with evil. John 3:16 says that God loves the whole world so much that He gave His Son to die for us. The Lord Jesus said, in John 10:10 that the thief comes to steal, kill and destroy, but Jesus said that He came to give us abundant life.

So, however you translate those verses I read in Deuteronomy 28, they must line up and agree with God's nature and character throughout the rest of His Word. Here is something else that will help you even if you did not know about causative and permissive verbs. When the writers pinned the 66 books of the Bible, they always recognized the Lord as Almighty God, the true and only God and the supreme Judge. Ultimately, everyone has to answer to Him. When those verses in Deuteronomy and other Scriptures say that God will send something bad upon you, they are simply acknowledging that the Judge of the universe determines what the verdict will be. The Judge (the Lord) did not make the curse come on Israel, the curse was already in the world, and Israel by their wrong choices allowed the curse to come into their lives.

The Judge (being God) simply told them what would happen to them as a result of their disobedience. If we say that God allowed it, that means He did not stop it from happening. As long as they stayed in faith, God's hand of protection held back the curse; when they got into fear, doubt and sin that caused God's hand of protection to be removed. You could say that the Judge told Israel what the choices were: life or death; curses or blessings, but they still had to choose. If you want the verdict or the final outcome to be a manifestation of blessings in your life, then choose blessings. When you believe and confess what the Word says about you, then your Father and Judge will make sure it comes to pass in your life.

I like to think about it this way. On this earth, in a natural courtroom setting, the judge always determines the verdict for the plaintiff and the defendant. If a man comes to trial that has murdered three people, and the judge sentences him to life in prison; the consequences of the man's sin (the act of murder) is not the judge's fault. Now, since he is the judge, he is the one who announces the verdict or the penalties which will be enforced upon the guilty man. After the trial is over, the headline in the newspaper may read, "Judge <u>sends</u> murderer to jail for life." I seriously doubt that the headline will say, "Judge <u>allows</u> murderer to go to jail for life." With the first headline, it sounds like it was the judge's fault that the man went to jail doesn't it?

If that man had not murdered those people would he still go to jail for life? No! It was not the judge's fault he went to jail, it was the man's fault; but the guilty man and his friends will probably blame the judge for his jail sentence. Many times people want to blame the judge for their problems, but all he did was to pronounce the verdict. Yes, you could say that the judge allowed the guilty man to go to jail, but that only means that the judge did not stop it from happening; it was not his fault.

If you open up a door to sickness, disease, lack, fear, depression and strife in your life, do not blame God for it! It is your fault; you opened the door that allowed the devil to bring his judgement (evil) upon you. Sickness, disease, poverty and the curse of the law are never God's judgements on anyone; because Jesus bore all of those judgements for us and freed us from them. If that kind of judgement comes into your life, it is coming from the devil. Just because the Lord (our Judge) told you in His Word that those things would come upon you through sin and disobedience does not mean it was His fault! Do not blame God for what you are going through! Stay in faith, love God with all your heart, and believe for Him to turn those bad situations around to work out for His glory and your good (Romans 8:26-28)!

Our Father in Heaven is always merciful! His grace, goodness and mercies endure forever! The great news for us today is that we are living under grace and our Lord Jesus took upon Himself all of our judgment at Calvary, paid our full penalty for the sin nature and all sins! He redeemed us and translated us

The Law of the Spirit of Life in Christ Jesus

into God's Kingdom and made us citizens of His household; the blessed of the Lord in Him!! It is time for every Believer to walk and live by the law of the Spirit of life in Christ Jesus! Release your faith today and expect to experience total freedom from every vestige of the law of sin and death in your life! Then, go forth and be the vessels of God's glory and power to the rest of the world!

If you would like to inquire for meetings with Dwayne and Leia, please send them an email to: dwayne7@att.net

If you desire to purchase any other of Dwayne's books or sow a financial seed, please visit their website at: dwaynenormanministries.org Thank You.

Also, if you would like to hear more teachings by Dwayne Norman, please tune into his internet radio program "Victory in the Word" on wofr.org Monday thru Friday at 4pm Eastern Standard time and Saturday at 7:30am Eastern Standard time. If you do not want to use the internet, you are welcome to dial (605) 477-5254 and listen to the program on your phone.

He has also downloaded about 300 messages onto the internet, just go onto youtube.com and type in Dwayne Norman to find them.

Other books by Dwayne Norman:

Are You Skilled in the Word of Righteousness?
Defending the Faith
Demonstrating God's Kingdom
God's Elijah Army
God's Will is Healing
Going Up to the High Place
Grace, Faith, Rest
How to Respond to a Bad Report
In Christ, True Purpose, True Peace, True Fulfillment
Just Believe
Resurrection Witnesses
The Awesome Power in the Message of the Cross
The Imposed Covenant
The Mystery
The Mystery Study Guide
The Prosperous Seed
True Repentance
Your Beginning with God

- Contemplation
- Preparation
- Action
- Maintenance

Intro — Recidivism vs Success
Thesis statement

① Recidivism
   - Definition
   - How its Measured
   - Faultiness
     - measures success of system, not individual
     - varies by state, no uniform measure
     - doesn't take all factors into consideration

② Success
   - Definition by Dr. Myles Munroe
   - How its measured
   - Guarantee success

Closing